An Introduction to the Homily

Robert P. Waznak, S.S.

A Liturgical Press Book

THE LITURGICAL PRESS
Collegeville, Minnesota

Cover design by David Manahan, O.S.B.

8

Library of Congress Cataloging-in-Publication Data

Waznak, Robert P.
    An introduction to the homily / Robert P. Waznak.
       p.   cm.
    Includes bibliographical references.
    ISBN 0-8146-2502-9 (alk. paper)
    1. Preaching. 2. Catholic preaching. I. Title.
  BV4211.2.W33   1998
  251–dc21   97-52989
                                          CIP

In loving memory of my parents—
Frank and Sophie Waznak

Acknowledgments

To my students, friends, and colleagues in various parish and educational settings I am grateful for the many insights I have received and which have contributed to this text. Particular thanks are due to colleagues and friends who read the manuscript and offered suggestions: James A. Wallace, C.Ss.R., Daniel P. Grigassy, O.F.M., John Allyn Melloh, S.M., Roland E. Murphy, O.Carm., Walter J. Burghardt, S.J., Joan Delaplane, O.P., and Ronald D. Witherup, S.S. I am also indebted to the librarian of Washington Theological Union, John S. Hanson, for his generous assistance. Finally, thanks are due to the president and board of trustees of WTU and the provincial council of the Society of St. Sulpice for granting me a sabbatical to complete this project.

Contents

Preface

Over three decades ago the bishops of the Second Vatican Council sparked the flames of a renewal of preaching in the life of the Church. The council made, what was then, some startling statements about the preaching ministry. Vatican II's Decree on the Ministry and Life of Priests *(Presbyterorum ordinis)* noted that the "primary duty" of priests was the "proclamation of the Gospel of God to all" (4). The Dogmatic Constitution on Divine Revelation *(Dei Verbum)* clearly signaled a return to the biblical foundations of preaching when it insisted that "all the preaching of the Church must be nourished and ruled by Sacred Scripture" (21). The Constitution on the Sacred Liturgy insisted that preaching was to "draw its content mainly from scriptural and liturgical sources" *(Sacrosanctum Concilium,* 35); the homily was to flow "from the sacred text" *(SC,* 52). To help assure a biblical preaching renewal, the council called for "a richer fare" of the Bible so that "a more representative part of the sacred scriptures will be read to the people in the course of a prescribed number of years" *(SC,* 51). This call resulted in the *Lectionary for Mass* (1969), a three-year cycle of scripture readings that replaced the one-year cycle of epistle and gospel readings of the *Missale Romanum* (1570). A sacramental theology of revelation that underscored the relation between the Liturgy of the Word and the Liturgy of the Eucharist found its way into the council's insistence on the "intimate connection between rites and words" *(SC,* 35). The homily was "to be highly esteemed as part of the liturgy itself" *(SC,* 52).

The above conciliar statements were startling when placed within the homiletic practice and literature of the time. In the early 1960s some liturgists were still calling the sermon an "interruption" of the

Mass or something "accidental" to the Mass. Here is how a liturgical historian described the worship sermon prior to Vatican II:

> Cut off from the liturgical action which it once developed and explained, the sermon developed into an independent and autonomous activity having no relation to anything else, much less to worship. The very content of preaching changed. From a proclamation of the Word of God (as it was in apostolic and patristic times) it became—and largely has remained—a thinly-disguised classroom lecture. More often than not it has little of the doctrinal about it, and it is confined mostly to moral exhortation.[1]

The Second Vatican Council, which restored the biblical form of preaching that had been an integral part of the liturgy of the early Church, did not have the final word on what a homily is and what it is supposed to accomplish. Hundreds of books and articles on preaching have appeared since Vatican II. Because homiletics never occupied a primary academic status in Roman Catholic theological education, most of these texts, especially the theoretical ones, have come from Protestant and Anglican homileticians. These homiletic texts rarely include the theological and liturgical insights from Catholic scholars and church documents such as the U.S. Bishops' document *Fulfilled in Your Hearing: The Homily in The Sunday Assembly* (1982). The renowned Presbyterian homiletician David G. Buttrick believes that "Protestant clergy are woefully ignorant of the theological changes that have taken place in Catholicism since Vatican II."[2] Conversely, contemporary Catholic homiletic literature often displays a lack of knowledge and appreciation of Protestant and Anglican homiletic scholarship, often referred to as "the New Homiletic." The purpose of this book is to demonstrate how the work of homiletic scholars from the various Christian Churches, the insights found in normative church documents, contemporary theological, liturgical, and biblical studies, plus the lived experiences of preachers and people can help us come to a clearer understanding of the function of the homily in the liturgical tradition of the Roman Catholic Church.

In the planning stages for preaching workshops, frequently I am asked to demonstrate the latest methods of preparing and delivering a homily. Those are worthwhile requests. But before we begin to demonstrate *how* to preach a homily, we need to explore *what* the homily is. That is why I have not attempted to write yet another "how to" book but a work that seeks to glean the pertinent literature in order to lead to a practical understanding of what the homily is and what it is supposed to do. Liturgical scholar Mary Collins has observed that "the lack of sound theory may underlie the chronic weakness in liturgical preaching that persists despite the church's conviction that the homily is a constitutive element of our eucharistic praxis."[3] This work is not written primarily for homileticians who seek new breakthroughs in their field but to provide "sound theory" for homilists striving to improve their preaching. Its design is synthetic. It is written as an introduction to the homily, especially for students, preachers, and liturgists in the Roman Catholic preaching tradition.

The bishops of Vatican II did not have an easy time defining the homily. They debated its source and purpose within the liturgical tradition. Some sought to retrieve the tradition of the early Church where the homily was a bridge that expounded the proclaimed biblical texts and led to prayer. Other bishops, however, were not comfortable with this retrieval of the biblical homily. They did not want to surrender the sermon which they viewed as an indispensable vehicle for expounding the teachings of the Church. In some Roman Catholic circles there seems to be a return to a pre-Vatican II instructional sermon rather than the liturgical homily proposed by the council. Some, worried about the people's ignorance of church teaching, see the liturgy as a convenient platform for doctrinal and moral instruction. This view could lead to a revival of pre-conciliar thought where the sermon was considered an "interruption" in the liturgy. Some theorists and preachers, devoted to the biblical foundation of the homily, seem to view it as an exegesis of the proclaimed readings with little thought given to the purpose of the liturgy which is the prayer and formation of the assembly. There is confusion about the role of the preacher's story in the homily. Some purists insist that there is no reason for a homilist to include personal stories since they tend to set up the preacher as the norm for the community's experience of faith and eclipse the story of God. Others blithely indulge in narcissistic preaching Sunday after Sunday since they claim it is what the people want. To help respond to these contemporary viewpoints, chapter 1 explores the particular form of preaching called the homily both from historical and contemporary understandings.

Normative documents and homiletic literature have always been concerned with the particular liturgical and cultural contexts of the homily. The so-called New Homiletic is a natural outgrowth of a phenomenological approach to preaching. It is an approach that reminds us of a remark made once by Karl Rahner: "The preacher should be able to hear his own sermon with the ears of his actual audience."[4] Homiletic textbooks have traditionally insisted on a logical form for the sermon that guaranteed focus and unity. But the traditional homiletic rubric of "tell them what you are going to say, tell them your message, and then tell them what they've just heard" has been challenged by the New Homiletic which recognizes other kinds of structures besides the deductive or Aristotelian. There are narrative, inductive, and metaphorical structures as well. Chapter 1 seeks to fill the void in many Catholic homiletic texts and popular articles on preaching by offering a brief overview of the New Homiletic.

One effective way to discover what the homily is supposed to do is to examine who the homilist is called to be. Chapter 2 presents an overview of the preacher from four major images within the Catholic homiletic tradition: the *herald,* the *teacher,* the *interpreter,* and the *witness.* The council retrieved the ancient image of the *herald* when it described preaching as "the proclamation of God's wonderful works in the history of salvation" (*SC,* 35). The image of the preacher as *teacher* was prominent in the Catholic Church from Trent to the Second Vatican Council. Vatican II still kept the image when it said that in the "homily the mysteries of the faith and the guiding principles of the Christian life are expounded . . . ." (*SC,* 52). Two more images of the preacher deserve our attention: the *interpreter* which is the prime image of *Fulfilled in Your Hearing* and the *witness* reintroduced by Pope Paul VI in his apostolic exhortation On Evangelization in the Modern World.[5] Chapter 2 will examine these four images, both for their strengths and for their shadow sides.

Methodist liturgical scholar James White has called the Roman Lectionary "Catholicism's greatest gift to Protestant preaching."[6] It was designed to give a "richer fare" of the Bible at the table of God's word (*SC,* 51). The lectionary readings serve the homily in the Catholic liturgical context of praise, remembering, and petitioning. That context is often ignored by preachers who think that their task is to explain the readings as one would do in a classroom. The Lectionary has proved to be a great blessing to the Church's liturgical life, but for some preachers there is still confusion about its purpose and plan. The Lectionary poses some particular problems for homilists, and some authors have offered suggestions for its improvement. Chapter 3 examines the origins of the Lectionary to help understand its place in the preaching event and explore some practical solutions to its problems.

I have spent the last twenty-five years teaching homiletics in theological schools, seminaries, and clergy workshops. From that experience I have gathered questions often asked concerning practical aspects about the homily. Chapter 4 attempts to provide some helpful responses to these questions.

This book concentrates primarily on the Sunday homily. The limitations of this book will not allow for a complete presentation of other forms of preaching, i.e., homilies for children, weddings, funerals, etc. I will, however, attend to certain features of these homilies in chapter 4.

Notes

1. William O'Shea, S.S., "The Sermon is Part of the Mass," *The Homiletic and Pastoral Review* (March 1960) 517.

2. David G. Buttrick, "Preaching the Lectionary: Two Cheers and Some Questions," *Reformed Liturgy and Music* (Spring 1994) 77.

3. Mary Collins, O.S.B., "Liturgical Homily: Connecting the Body," *Eucharist: Toward the Third Millennium,* ed. Gerard Austin (Chicago: Liturgical Training Publications, 1997) 88.

4. Karl Rahner, S.J., "Demythologization and the Sermon," ed. Karl Rahner, *The Renewal of Preaching: Theory and Practice,* Concilium, vol. 33, trans. Theodore L. Weston (New York: Paulist Press, 1968) 25.

5. Pope Paul VI, *On Evangelization in the Modern World* (Washington, D.C.: United States Catholic Conference, 1976) 41.

6. James White, *Christian Worship in Transition* (Nashville: Abingdon, 1976) 139.

1

From Sermon to Homily

Roman Catholics generally use "homily" to name the renewed form of preaching initiated by the liturgical reforms of the Second Vatican Council. It is that form of preaching which flows from and immediately follows the scriptural readings of the liturgy and which leads to the celebration of the sacraments. In current Catholic parlance "homily" is distinguished from "sermon" where the latter names a form of preaching that is not necessarily connected to the biblical and liturgical texts and is heard outside the context of the liturgy. Many use "sermon" to describe pre-Vatican II preaching and "homily" to refer to the kind of preaching envisioned by the council.

But these distinctions are not always found outside the Roman Church. We cannot rely, for example, on popular dictionaries to give us a working definition for the word "homily." For some, it is a biblical sermon; for others, a doctrinal talk. Some dictionaries claim that the aim of the homily is to edify a congregation; others give as its purpose moral instruction. There are traces of a negative connotation of homily in the English language since at least Shakespeare's time. In *As You Like It,* Duke Senior speaks eloquently of "sermons in stones, and good in everything."[1] But later on in the play Rosalind laments, "O most gentle Jupiter, what tedious homily of love have you wearied your parishioners withal . . . ."[2] This tradition continues in our own day when secular discourse seems to give a more negative connotation to homily than to sermon. Homily is often used to describe a pious little talk. This is reflected in the third meaning of the word in *Webster's College Dictionary* (1991): "an inspirational saying or cliché."

Even among the Christian Churches there is diversity of use. Protestants still prefer the word "sermon," even when they refer to preaching that occurs within the liturgy.[3] When they do use the term, it is sometimes described in the patristic preaching tradition as a "walking through the text, step by step."[4] In *Design for Preaching,* a homiletic textbook used for generations in many Protestant seminaries, Henry Grady Davis described the word "homily" in chameleon terms:

> The *homily* is not a definite sermonic form. In its early phase, it was an informal, discursive talk, in which digression, passing from one subject to another, was rather the rule than the exception. The early homily used no text and developed no particular theme. Later in the history of preaching, the term came to mean almost the opposite: an ordered exposition of a passage of Scripture. The hundreds of sermons by Chrysostom, Augustine, and the other fathers, have come down to us as "homilies" in this latter sense. The term is not useful for our purposes.[5]

Presbyterian pastor Donald Wilson Stake finds no meaningful distinction between a sermon and a homily. In the entry "homily" of his liturgical dictionary he writes: "Roman Catholics generally use this term, while Protestants opt for the word 'sermon.' The two words mean the same thing, namely the proclamation of the Word."[6]

Anglican homiletician Charles L. Rice makes a distinction between what he calls the "concise homily" and the "extended sermon." Rice notes that Roman Catholics and, to a lesser degree, Anglicans are accustomed to concise homilies at the Eucharist: "If the Communion is to be celebrated properly, there usually is not time for an extended sermon."[7] For Rice the brief homily, which he describes as "a comment on the connection of one or more of the texts to the liturgical occasion is 'liturgy-friendly' . . . [it] must rely on the liturgical occasion for its power."[8]

Retrieval of an Ancient Preaching Term

Charles Rice's insistence on the liturgical context of the homily resonates with contemporary Roman Catholic usage of the word. Even though canon 1344 of the 1918 *The Code of Canon Law* used the term *consueta homilia* (the usual homily), the word "homily" was not part of ordinary Catholic parlance prior to the Second Vatican Council. The council's Constitution on the Sacred Liturgy used the word to describe the kind of preaching that takes place at liturgy: "The homily, therefore, is to be highly esteemed as part of the liturgy itself" (*SC,* 52). The bishops sought to restore this form of preaching which had been an integral part of the liturgy in the ancient Church where exhortation followed the Scriptures proclaimed and led to the eucharistic meal. That tradition is first recorded in the mid-second century *First Apology* of Justin Martyr:

> On the day which is called Sunday we have a common assembly of all who live in the cities or in the outlying districts, and the memoirs of the Apostles or the writings of the Prophets are read, as long as there is time. Then, when the reader has finished, the president of the assembly verbally admonishes and invites all to imitate such examples of virtue. Then we all stand up together and offer up our prayers, and, as we said before, after we finish our prayers, bread and wine and water are presented. He who presides likewise offers up prayers and thanksgivings, to the best of his ability, and the people express their approval by saying "Amen." The Eucharistic elements are distributed and consumed by those present and to those who are absent they are sent through the deacons.[9]

The council's retrieval of the patristic notion of the homily was influenced by the convergence of the biblical, liturgical, theological, and catechetical scholarship of the time. The scientific critical study of the Bible that appeared in Catholic circles at the end of the nineteenth century received papal approbation in Pope Pius XII's *Divino Afflante Spiritu* in 1943. The fruits of modern methods of biblical interpretation are found throughout the sixteen documents of the Second Vatican Council. A Protestant observer, Oscar Cullmann, remarked that the "Catholic Church in Vatican II not only goes back behind the Counter-Reformation, but even behind the Middle Ages. It goes back to the Bible."[10] The Pauline doctrine of the Body of Christ developed by contemporary biblical scholars and the insights of the vigorous liturgical movement pioneered in the monasteries of northern Europe at the beginning of this century found their place in Pius XII's *Mediator Dei* (1947). This encyclical, which called for active participation in worship and emphasized the relationship of liturgy and life, helped provide the liturgical framework for Vatican II's document on the sacred liturgy. The sacramental theology of revelation proposed by Karl Rahner, Otto Semmelroth, Yves Congar, Michael Schmaus, Charles Davis, and Edward Schillebeeckx contributed a renewed understanding of the relation between the Liturgy of the Word and the Eucharist. For these theologians, the sacraments were inconceivable without preaching. They were influenced by the so-called kerygmatic movement of their day which emphasized the announcement of the Good News. They, therefore, stressed preaching as a proclamation of the saving events celebrated at the table of the Lord. Vatican II insisted that a kerygmatic character should permeate the homily. The Constitution on the Sacred Liturgy highlighted "the proclamation of God's wonderful works in the history of salvation" (*SC,* 35).

Despite the powerful influences of biblical, liturgical, theological, and catechetical scholarship of the day, not all council bishops were eager to return to the tradition of the early Church where the homily was a bridge that expounded the proclaimed Scriptures and led to prayer. Some bishops were uneasy with a retrieval of the biblical homily. They wanted *SC* to make it clear that preaching at Mass should concern itself with all aspects of the Christian faith and argued for the use of the term "catechesis" or "sermon" instead of "homily." These bishops called for a syllabus of catechetical instruction to govern what was preached; they urged the teaching of all Christian doctrine over a period of four to five years based on liturgical texts. This catechetical approach of preaching doctrine and morals had been entrenched in Catholic preaching since the Council of Trent. Many of the sermons heard before Vatican II had little or no reference to the scripture readings proclaimed at Mass. The debate about the character of liturgical preaching resulted in an ambivalence within *SC* when at times the word "homily" is used and at other times "sermon."

In choosing the word "homily" to describe the preaching event of a renewed liturgy, the bishops retrieved a term that had ancient origins. While the word homily *(homilia)* is not used in the New Testament, we do find the Greek verb, *homilein,* which implies a familiar conversation. For example, Cleopas and his friend, who traveled from Jerusalem to Emmaus, were "talking with each other *(homiloun)* about all these things that had happened" (Luke 24:14). It was Origen (185–254) who for the first time in Christian usage supplied a definition to the word "homily." He called his thirty-nine discourses on Luke *homiliai.* They (1) were preached in a liturgy, (2) had a prophetic quality, (3) were based on a running or continuous exposition of the biblical text, and (4) were conversational in tone. Origen's pastoral zeal for the spiritual needs of the people was more important to him than the exaggerated rhetoric of his day (the Second Sophistic). He made a distinction between *logos* or *sermo* and *homilia* or *tractatus*. *Logos* followed the shape of classical rhetoric, while the form of *homilia* was direct and free. *Homilia* was a popular, allegorical exposition and application of Scripture.[11] It had its roots in the hermeneutical practice of *midrash haggadah* or narrative expansion that commented on Scripture through imaginative instruction and exhortation.

We must not think that because Origen's style was familiar conversation rather than the formal rhetoric of his contemporaries, that his homilies did not contain structure. Joseph T. Lienhard's analysis of Origen's homilies illustrates that although they lacked rhetorical flare, there was structure:

> They were utterly lacking in rhetorical polish, and showed the simplicity that led the church to choose to call discourses on the scriptures *homilia*. After the reading, and with little or no introduction, Origen would begin to explain the scripture, verse by verse. He dealt first with the literal sense, then with any spiritual senses he discovered. He always tried to find a way for his hearers to apply the passage to their lives. He ended his homilies, sometimes quite abruptly, with a doxology.[12]

Lienhard maintains that the distinctive characteristic of a homily by Origen was "its apparent artlessness, which marked the homily off from the studied and stylized speech" of his day.[13] It was similar to the *homilia* or the kind of instruction that a philosopher would give his pupils: a familiar conversation. That is why Henry Grady Davis' characterization of the early homily as a meandering talk that had no "text and developed no particular theme" is a harsh and sweeping judgment.

For Origen the homily meant a type of preaching within the liturgy that related to the great events of salvation history. The homily was "a mutual search by preacher and congregation—a seeking after the voice of God."[14] Origen was a preacher devoted to interpreting the Bible. He was especially concerned with the spiritual interpretation of Scripture. In preaching on Leviticus 1:4 (about the skinning of the carcass of a sacrificial animal) Origen could say, "I myself think that the priest . . . is the one who removes the veil of the letter from the word of God and uncovers its interior parts which are members of spiritual understanding."[15]

The homilies of the eastern Fathers of the second and third centuries interpreted the Scriptures to show that Christ was as present in the biblical readings as he was in the eucharistic meal. These homilies still resembled the synagogue practice of informal preaching.

In the fourth century preaching began to become more formalized. There were a number of reasons for this change: the differentiation between the Mass of the catechumens and the Mass of the faithful began to be more sharply emphasized, and thus a need for catechetical preaching arose; the birth of new liturgical seasons and feast days of saints and martyrs changed the tone of the homily; the need to fight heresies brought about apologetic discourses in defense of the faith; interest in classical rhetoric introduced new oratorical devices. St. Augustine (354–430) described the Bible as a kind of classic rhetoric. Book IV of his *De Doctrina Christiana* employed Ciceronian rhetorical principles for Christian preaching. Augustine, a former teacher of rhetoric, deplored the poorly fashioned homilies of his day and encouraged preachers to learn the technical devices of persuasive rhetoric. Rhetorical elaboration is found, for example, in Augustine's sermon on St. Lawrence, Deacon and Martyr:

> I tell you again and again, my brethren, that in the Lord's garden are to be found not only the roses of the martyrs. In it there are also the lilies of the virgins, the ivy of wedded couples, and the violets of widows. On no account may any class of people despair, thinking that God has not called them. Christ suffered for all.[16]

Preaching began to develop biblical or theological themes for the catechetical instruction of those seeking baptism and also mystagogical instruction (initiation into the mysteries of Christ as revealed in the sacraments) to those who were recently baptized. The great homilies of the fourth-century Fathers were not always preached after the gospel at Mass. They were preached at almost any point in the sequence of services. St. John, patriarch of Constantinople (350–407), who was known as "Chrysostom" or the golden mouth, preached his series of homilies on Genesis toward the day's end, before evening prayer or vespers. In some Palestinian churches, not only the bishop preached at Mass, but all his assisting senior clergy preached after him in sequence. The homily, therefore, took a considerable length of time, becoming almost a service of its own. It is reported that Chrysostom preached at times for over two hours while his listeners wept, cheered, applauded, and pounded their breasts.

After the time of Augustine and Chrysostom, a decline in preaching occurred. The Divine Liturgy in the East became viewed as a mystical sacrifice in which the homily had difficulty finding its proper place. Preaching turned from an actualization of a biblical passage to an explanation of a certain doctrine or event. Funeral discourses, panegyrics for the martyrs, and theological orations and eulogies on the Mother of God became popular. In the West, the homily of the primitive Church became dominated by elaborate ritual. The sermons of Pope Leo the Great (+461) are liturgical since they are expositions of biblical passages of the recently completed liturgical cycle but they do not reflect the prophetic quality of Origen, Chrysostom, or Augustine. Leo's sermons are more thematic than exegetical since he sought to preach a dogmatic defense of Chalcedon's doctrine in opposition to the Monophysites. Leo's sermons do not possess a quality of familiar conversation since he loved the rhetorical devices of his time: antithesis, assonance, and rhythmical cadences.

Pope Gregory the Great's (540?–604) liturgical reforms embellished ceremonies but lessened the importance of a prophetic and imaginative interpretation of the Scriptures. Yngve Brilioth remarks that while the reforms strongly supported preaching within the context of the Mass, "the solicitude for the cult itself, to which Gregory contributed mightily, became the chief enemy of preaching in the Roman church."[17] His reforms actually promoted the practice of reading at the liturgy the homily of some revered teacher from the past. Thus, the prophetic quality of preaching, which emphasized the unique circumstances and times of a particular congregation, was dampened. While we still use the word "homily" to describe the preaching of the Fathers of the Church, by the end of the patristic era preaching lost the quality of an informal interpretation of the Scriptures as found in Justin Martyr's *First Apology* or the familiar conversational tone of Origen's preaching. By the late Middle Ages "[t]he old fashioned parish sermon in the mass dies out and with it, perhaps also the artless pattern of the homily."[18]

One can find many instances in the Church's history when great preachers and new movements kept preaching alive. Valiant attempts were also made by church authorities to ensure that the gospel would be preached faithfully and effectively. But there were also many forces that militated against the biblical, liturgical, kerygmatic, homiletic, and prophetic aspects of the homily. For example, the twelfth and thirteenth centuries witnessed the revival of preaching by the Dominicans and Franciscans. With these mendicant orders, preaching became more popular and of better quality. But the scholastic sermon favored by the Dominicans was often complicated and aimed at the defense of the faith against heresies. Popular preaching of the Franciscans often used biblical texts as convenient hooks for moral exhortation to religious practices.[19]

Countless collections of sermon aids provided preachers with allegorical material for biblical exegesis, scholarly quotations from the literature of antiquity, and bizarre stories, legends and illustrations. The prophetic aspect of the homily which opened up the Scriptures and demanded a response from listeners was threatened by these homiletic aids. Brilioth observes that the entire period from the collapse of the western Roman Empire to the Reformation was one in which "preaching had become an art in the use of borrowed materials."[20]

On the eve of the Reformation, the Fifth Lateran Council attempted a preaching renaissance. On December 19, 1516, it issued a decree which emphatically stated that preaching should concern itself with the gospel and not with "imminent events, apocalyptic messages, preposterous stories, fabulous miracles, arcane trivia, heretical opinions and downright nonsense."[21] The decree did not seem to forestall the ills of poor preaching. Thirty years later the Council of Trent sought a similar reform by directing preachers

> . . . to preach the holy Gospel of Jesus Christ . . . to feed the people committed to them with wholesome words in proportion to their own and their people's capacity, by teaching them those things that are necessary for all to know in order to be saved, and by impressing upon them with briefness and plainness of speech the vices that they must avoid and the virtues that they must cultivate, in order that they may escape eternal punishment and obtain the glory of heaven.[22]

The Counter-Reformation's renewal of preaching did not restore the homily of the early Church. In focusing on vices and virtues, Trent borrowed from the tradition of St. Francis of Assisi (1182–1226) who urged his friars to penetrate the hearts of their listeners by edification and definition of virtues and vices.[23] This theme is also found in Augustine when he defined the "end" of preaching: "that good habits be loved and evil avoided."[24] The mission of post-Tridentine preachers was "to move sinners to repentance, to move *(movere)* the will, to bring about contrition and satisfaction, to effect moral reform and a return to the Church's channels of grace."[25]

Twenty years after Trent's decree on preaching came the *Catechism of the Council of Trent,* often referred to as the "Roman Catechism." It provided sermon material not only on the themes of vices and virtues but "those things that are necessary for all to know in order to be saved." St. Robert Bellarmine taught that "the aim of the Christian preacher should be to teach what the faithful should know or what is fitting for them to know of divine doctrine, and at the same time to move them to attain virtues and flee vices."[26]

Preachers were advised not to use the material in the catechism in the form of the traditional "scholastic" sermon but as proclamation and authority. But this Tridentine ideal was not always honored. The *Roman Catechism* divided up its treatment of "those things necessary" into the twelve articles of the Creed, the seven sacraments, the ten commandments, prayer, and the Lord's Prayer. This division provided a convenient tract for preachers to follow.

Prior to the preaching reforms of the Second Vatican Council, many dioceses in the United States provided homiletic syllabi containing this division of doctrinal and moral topics that were totally unrelated to the scriptural readings of the Mass. A popular homiletic textbook used in Catholic seminaries prior to the council reflects how the instructional preaching of the day had eclipsed the biblical and liturgical traditions of the early Church:

> The canonical idea of a sermon does not include the text as essential to the sermon, for a sermon is defined by Father McVann in "The Canon Law on Sermon Preaching," as "a sacred public address, given by one duly empowered by the Church, and intended to instruct its listeners in the Christian faith and move them to practice it." The sermon need not begin with a text then.[27]

Liturgical scholars who called for a return to the homily of the early Church during Vatican II frequently lamented the instructional sermons of the day which were nothing more than boring lectures on threadbare truths from the *Roman Catechism* or a catechetical text book, or moral harangues topped off with a bit of *ferverino*. While not advocating that homilies be devoid of theological content and church teaching, these scholars placed primary emphasis on the biblical, liturgical, and kerygmatic aspects of the homily.

Refinement of an Ancient Term

Over the past three decades liturgists, homileticians, and church documents have attempted to advance a contemporary understanding of the homily. Not long after *SC* was promulgated, refinements of the homily were made in conciliar and post-conciliar decrees. Most of these favored the renewed understanding of the liturgical homily of the early Church rather than the instructional sermon that followed the reforms of the Council of Trent. *Presbyterorum ordinis* advised that today's preaching "must expound the Word of God not merely in a general and abstract way but by an application of the eternal truth of the gospel to the concrete circumstances of life" (4). *Dei Verbum* highlighted the biblical foundations of preaching when it said that "all the preaching of the church must be nourished and ruled by Sacred Scripture" (21). The earliest instruction on the implementation of *SC* said that the homily "means an explanation pertinent to the mystery celebrated and the special needs of the listeners of some point in either the readings from sacred Scripture or in another text from the Ordinary or Proper of the day's Mass" (*Inter oecumenici, 54*).

In 1970, the General Instruction of the Roman Missal *(Cenam Paschalem)* stated something quite similar about the homily: "Its content should be an exposition of the scripture readings or of some particular aspect of them, or of some other text taken from the Order or the Proper of the Mass for the day, having regard for the mystery being celebrated or the special needs of those who hear it" (41). Six months after *CP*, the Third Instruction on the Correct Implementation of the Constitution *(Liturgiae instaurationes)* stated: "The purpose of the homily is to explain the readings and make them relevant for the present day" (2, a). In the *Lectionary for Mass: General Introduction,* we read:

> Whether the homily explains the biblical word of God proclaimed in the readings or some other text of the liturgy, it must always lead the community of the faithful to celebrate the Eucharist wholeheartedly . . . But this demands that the homily be truly the fruit of meditation, carefully prepared, neither too long nor too short, and suited to all those present, even children and the uneducated (24).

These church documents emphasized the biblical, liturgical, kerygmatic, homiletic, and prophetic aspects of the homily. The prophetic aspect is not found in *SC*'s description of the homily. Three years after *SC* was promulgated, Godfrey Diekmann remarked that one of the weaknesses of the constitution was that it failed "to correlate liturgical action to the other areas of Christian life, whether devotional or apostolic."[28] While the documents that followed *SC* do not use the term "prophetic" to describe the homily, the prophetic aspect is present in such phrases as the "concrete circumstances of life," "needs proper to the listeners," and "relevant for the present day." And while the documents do not use the term "familiar conversation" to describe the new homiletic of Vatican II, the mark of "familiar conversation" rather than theoretical instruction is present in such phrases as "preaching must not present God's Word in a general and abstract fashion only" and the homily should be "neither too long nor too short, and suited to all those present, even children and the uneducated."

Liturgical scholars continued to refine definitions of the homily by stressing its biblical, liturgical, kerygmatic, homiletic, and prophetic aspects. Speaking at the North American Liturgical Week in the same year that *SC* was promulgated (1963), Gerard Sloyan advised:

> Keep your eye always on the kerygma, the central core of the Gospel that contains in summary the terms of our salvation. Proclaim the meaning of this Gospel of today in relation to it. At the same time, relate your proclamation to this assembly, this feast, these people's lives in Feasterville, Pennsylvania.[29]

William Skudlarek describes the homily as "an integral part of the liturgical action in which the words of Scripture are used to interpret the lives of the people in such a way that they are enabled to participate in the liturgical action with faith."[30] He examines the way in which the verb *homilein* is used in the New Testament and concludes that it was more conversational in tone than that employed by the ancient Greek orators. Skudlarek thus argues that the homily is addressed not to "some haphazard conglomerate of anonymous strangers, but a gathering of friends, people with whom one is familiar and to whom one can speak comfortably and easily."[31]

But in a book aimed mostly at Roman Catholics, Anglican homiletician O.C. Edwards, Jr. discourages speculation about the meaning of homily as familiar conversation: "Some scholars have tried to break down the etymology of homily into its original Greek components and thus suggested that it means 'communication with a crowd' but surely this is the etymological fallacy of assuming that the present meaning of a word is governed by the roots from which it was derived."[32] Since the Greek *homilia* and the Latin *sermo* both have the same sense of conversation, talk, or discussion, Edward's point is well made. But Skudlarek's emphasis on the familiar conversational quality of preaching is worthy of our attention. In a popular nineteenth-century homiletic textbook, Baptist preacher John Broadus also high-lighted the familiar conversational quality of the preaching of the early Church—whether they were called homilies or sermons—when he made the observation that "the early Christians did not apply to their public teachings the names given to the orations of Demosthenes and Cicero, but called them *talks,* familiar discourses."[33]

Joseph Gelineau adds to the discussion by insisting that the "primary function of the homily is prophecy, in the New Testament sense, that is to say the proclamation of God's intervention in Jesus Christ. 'Today this happens for me, for you, for us' . . . This word is also an example and encouragement given to the rest of the assembly."[34] Gelineau's comments remind us of Vatican II's description of a "proclamation of God's wonderful works in the history of salvation, which is the mystery of Christ ever made present and active in us, especially in the celebration of the liturgy" (*SC,* 35). They also echo the synagogue practice where sermons ended with words of consolation from references to the messianic age.[35]

Contemporary Roman Catholic liturgical scholars continue to derive their definition of the homily from reflection upon the seminal statement of *SC* that the homily is "part of the liturgy itself." Thus, Gerard Sloyan comments:

> The homily . . . is primarily worship or praise which is also thanksgiving and petition, like the total liturgical act. Commentary on the word does not stand apart from the remainder of the divine service; it is not different from it in kind. The eucharistic act praises God for the deed done on our behalf in Jesus Christ through the power of the Holy Spirit. The homily must do that as much as the biblical readings, the eucharistic prayer (the "canon" or "anaphora") and the communion rite.[36]

Kevin Irwin has argued for a careful nuancing of the conventional distinction which asserts that the word leads to sacrament. He observes that "the Word and sacrament are so essentially joined that they form one act of worship."[37] That one act of worship where we praise and give thanks to God is centered on what God has done for us *(anamnesis),* especially in the paschal mystery of Christ and petitioning or evoking *(epiclesis)* the Holy Spirit to continue to be present to us. The liturgy is accomplished by, with, and in the Church assembled in prayer which draws the faithful into a new experience of the redemptive acts of Christ and the longing for redemption's eschatological fulfillment in the kingdom. Irwin's understanding of the one act of worship leads him to state:

> The homily is an interpretation of the Scriptures in order that their anamnetic character can be unleashed in contemporary ecclesial settings . . . The move from Word to sacrament is established theologically and liturgically as more of a bridge than a leap because of their similarity as disclosive of the paschal mystery.[38]

A Shift from Explanation to Interpretation

The church document that has offered the most creative understanding of the liturgical homily since it was first proposed by Vatican II is an American product. *Fulfilled in Your Hearing: the Homily in the Sunday Assembly* came from the National Catholic Conference of Bishops' Committee on Priestly Life and Ministry (1982). This document summarizes the understandings of the homily as found in conciliar and post-conciliar documents and the liturgical literature since Vatican II that we have just reviewed:

> The very meaning and function of the homily is determined by its relation to the liturgical action of which it is a part. It flows from the Scriptures which are read at that liturgical celebration, or more broadly, from the Scriptures which undergird its prayers and actions, and it enables the congregation to participate in the celebrations with faith.[39]

But *FIYH* advances an understanding of the homily for our time by highlighting the "reading the signs of the times" motif from The Constitution on the Church in the Modern World. *Interpretation* is the key word in *FIYH*:

> Since the purpose of the homily is to enable the gathered congregation to celebrate the liturgy with faith, the preacher does not so much attempt to explain the Scriptures as to interpret the human situation through the Scriptures. In other words, the goal of the liturgical preacher is not to interpret a text of the Bible (as would be the case in teaching a Scripture class) as much as to draw on the texts of the Bible as they are presented in the lectionary to interpret people's lives. To be even more precise, the preacher's purpose will be to turn to these Scriptures to interpret people's lives in such a way that they will be able to celebrate Eucharist—or be reconciled with

God and with one another, or be baptized into the Body of Christ, depending on the particular liturgy that is being celebrated (20, 21).

FIYH defines the homily as "a scriptural interpretation of human existence which enables a community to recognize God's active presence, to respond to that presence in faith through liturgical word and gesture, and beyond the liturgical assembly, through a life lived in conformity with the Gospel" (29). The homilist is described as a "mediator of meaning." In other words, the homilist is primarily an interpreter, not a teacher. A teacher tells people what they do not know; an interpreter tells them what they already suspect or wonder about but have no words nor images for. The NCCB document reads the "signs of the times" and concludes that people today are "hungry, sometimes desperately so, for meaning in their lives." As "mediator of meaning,"

> The preacher represents this community by voicing its concerns by naming its demons, and thus enabling it to gain some understanding and control of the evil which afflicts it. He represents the Lord by offering the community another word, a word of healing and pardon, of acceptance and love (7).

FIYH offers a fresh understanding of the homily since it shifts its meaning from instruction to interpretation. Even though conciliar and post-conciliar documents describe the homily as a "proclamation of God's wonderful works in the history of salvation," they use instructional verbs to describe what the homilist is. *SC* states: "By means of the homily the mysteries of the faith and the guiding principles of the Christian life are expounded from the sacred text during the course of the liturgical year" (52). *The Code of Canon Law* (1983) draws upon this paragraph to supply a definition of the homily as expounding the mysteries of the faith and the norms of Christian living (Canon 767.1). The Code locates the homily in the "Book on the Teaching Office of the Church." The 1980 Roman Instruction on Certain Norms Concerning the Worship of the Eucharistic Mystery states that the purpose of the homily is "to explain to the faithful the word of God proclaimed in the readings, and to apply its message to the present" (3). This emphasis on *expounding* and *explaining* is also found in definitions of the homily by contemporary authors. Dennis Smolarski describes the homily as "[a]n explanation of the scriptural readings or of the feast given by an ordained minister during a liturgy."[40] O.C. Edwards, Jr. states that the homily "applies a point of doctrine drawn from that day's gospel to the lives of the members of the congregation."[41]

FIYH made a dramatic shift from the instructional language of explanation and application to a description of the homily as an interpretive act. This new shift, from an interpretation of Scripture with an application to life, to an interpretation of the human situation through Scripture, echoes contemporary christology with the mystery of the word "from below" rather than "from above." The new shift also helps us to name grace not only in the liturgy, but in our world of limitations. It should be noted here that the language of interpretation, found in the definition of the homily by William Skudlarek quoted above, made its way into *FIYH,* since Skudlarek was the principal author of the bishops' document.

Some Conclusions

We have seen that it is no easy task to define the word "homily." Just as there is a wide range of the meaning of homily in popular dictionaries, so there is a wide range of nuance in church documents and liturgical literature. The nature of the homily continues to be a topic of reflection decades after its reintroduction by the Second Vatican Council. The Constitution on the Sacred Liturgy sought to reform the Church's liturgy in order to renew the Church's life. That is clear from its opening lines: "The sacred Council has set out to impart an ever-increasing vigor to the Christian life of the faithful; to adapt more closely to the needs of our age" (*SC,* 1). The bishops chose the word "homily" not just because it had ancient roots but because they wished to name a renewed type of preaching for the liturgical assembly.

We can always benefit from a reexamination of our homiletic roots, not because our ancestors in the faith were perfect preachers, but because they offer us a perspective different from our own, and one that is closer to the preaching from which our faith and theology first sprang. But we must not think that we can locate one ideal form of the homily in history that will absolutely fulfill the needs of Christians today. Paul Bradshaw cautions against romanticizing the patristic era as the perfect liturgical age. He believes that one of the best lessons we can learn from that period "is that, whatever attempts were made to define and establish norms and conventions, pastoral practices broke through them all as it tried to respond to changing cultural patterns, pastoral needs, and theological trends."[42] That is why we must pay attention not only to the rich tradition of the homily in the early Church and the retrieval of this preaching form by Vatican II but also to the evolving understandings of the homily from those who have tried to respond to the changing cultural patterns, pastoral needs, and theological trends of our day. Mary Collins reminds us that "restoration is not mere imitation":

> The church of the apostles and the church of classical antiquity went beyond available forms of oral discourse, transforming available language to preach Christ Jesus and the dawning reign of God. On the edge of the third Christian millennium, we must emulate their project, not their product.[43]

Five Characteristics of the Homily

Our study has revealed five characteristics of preaching that were restored from the ancient tradition by Vatican II's retrieval of the homily: (1) *biblical*, (2) *liturgical*, (3) *kerygmatic*, (4) *conversational*, and, (5) *prophetic*. We will now reflect on these characteristics in light of contemporary understandings.

1) *Biblical*

Vatican II's renewal of the homily signaled a return to biblical preaching. "All the preaching of the Church, as indeed the entire Christian religion, should be nourished and ruled by Sacred Scripture" (*DV,* 21). Preaching always demands a method of biblical interpretation. *Dei Verbum* advocated the historical-critical method when it urged interpreters to "carefully search out the meaning which the sacred writers really had in mind" (12). At the time that the Church was calling for biblical preaching, scholars were producing new biblical commentaries like *The Jerome Biblical Commentary* that utilized the historical-critical method. Supply seemed to meet demand.

While historical-critical scholarship provided necessary and helpful parameters and insights for constructing a convincing homily, preachers soon learned that it is not enough to deal only with historical or scientific questions of biblical texts. The symbolic, evocative, and existential perception of the text is also required for preaching. The Church never had one method of interpreting the Scriptures.

Borrowing from the synagogue tradition, biblical readings were read and listened to not only out of intellectual curiosity but for existential reasons.

Much of the Bible originated in the worship of Israel and of the early Church. One of the most important criteria in the Church's formation of the canon was the liturgical use of a given book of the Bible. Geoffrey Wainwright has eloquently stressed the life-giving power of the Scriptures because of their proclamation in the liturgy:

> The worshipping community supplies a living continuity down the centuries for transmitting the great images and themes of the Scriptures which might otherwise have become unintelligible through external cultural changes. The constant features and qualitative wholeness of the liturgy also provide the stability and unity within which to come to terms with the highly diverse material of the Bible.[44]

We are encouraged to utilize all the available modern methods to interpret the biblical texts in the preparation of the homily. In the 1993 document of The Pontifical Biblical Commission, *The Interpretation of the Bible in the Church,* the historical-critical method is still referred to as "the indispensable method for the scientific study of the meaning of the ancient texts."[45] But there is an interesting admission in the 1993 document about "many members of the faithful, who judge the method [historical-critical] deficient from the point of view of faith."[46] The document emphasizes the necessity of *actualization* that "allows the Bible to remain fruitful at different periods" and *inculturation* which "ensures that the biblical message take root in a great variety of terrain."[47] Attention, therefore, is given to the value of literary analysis, canonical criticism, sociological, anthropological and psychological approaches, and the contextual approaches of liberationists and feminists.

The various "new" methods of biblical interpretation that have gained popularity since the Second Vatican Council can greatly assist us in preparing a biblical homily. However, in the actual preaching of the homily, we must remember that our task is not to interpret the biblical texts as we would in a Bible class. Our task is to interpret the human situation of the gathered assembly in light of the Good News of the scriptural texts proclaimed in the liturgy of the Church. This interpretation includes study but also faith, prayer, and meditation. While *FIYH* insists that homilists make use of the best biblical tools and methods in their study of the Bible, it also states that homilists "are called to a prayerful dwelling with their people and to a prayerful dwelling with the texts of the Scripture knowing them and allowing themselves to be known by them" (11). The homily is not a biblical lecture but a biblical interpretation of the life addressed to a particular liturgical assembly in a particular place and time.

2) *Liturgical*

Vatican II's statement that the homily is "part of the liturgy itself" (*SC*, 52) was meant to counteract the pre-conciliar belief that the homily was an interruption in the Mass. In the early 1960s some liturgists were referring to the homily as an "interruption" in the liturgy rather than an integral part of it. Some handbooks of moral theology considered missing the "Foremass" (what we now describe as the Liturgy of the Word) a "venial" sin, since it was not significant.[48] Such thinking revealed a loss of appreciation of the teaching and practice of the early Church that the Liturgy of the Word and the Liturgy of the Eucharist constitute one single act of worship.

The homily is not just a "part of the liturgy itself" but must also be part of the particular context of people's lives. In the *Lectionary for Mass: General Introduction* we read that the homily "must always lead the community of the faithful to celebrate the Eucharist wholeheartedly, 'so that they may hold fast in their lives to what they have grasped by their faith'" (24). *FIYH* states that the purpose of the homily is to enable "a community to recognize God's active presence, to respond to that presence in faith through liturgical word and gesture, and beyond the liturgical assembly, through a life lived in conformity with the Gospel" (29). In the Roman Catholic tradition the primary liturgical symbol is the assembly. *FIYH* recognizes that in the Church, as in every other gathering, there is a necessity to have offices and ministries but states that these are secondary. "The primary reality is Christ in the assembly, the People of God" (4).

A fascinating interplay takes place between liturgical and cultural contexts. In the early Church the main structure of the liturgy remained the same but, as Kevin Irwin points out, there was "a decided interplay and variability of liturgical forms, texts and explanations depending on contemporary controversies and local circumstances."[49] The homily could challenge the very meaning of why a particular group of people are assembled for worship. Geoffrey Wainwright has remarked:

> Surrounded as it is by the stable and well-tried elements of the scripture readings, the creed and the anaphora, the unrepeatable sermon can afford a certain boldness of mind and heart as it seeks to bring home the Christian message imaginatively and penetratingly to a particular group of people at this time and in this place.[50]

While the homily provides a bold and existential proclamation to the stability of the liturgy, the stability of liturgical ritual gives the homily its rootedness in the Gospel and the Church's tradition of prayer. Contemporary studies have highlighted the importance of ritual in the development, integration, and nurturing of the human person and the community.[51]

The stability of the liturgical context safeguards the homily from becoming an instruction, a harangue, a non-gospel speech, an appeal for personal piety over against the needs of the community. The very structure of ritual with its observable repetitiveness is a splendid counterpoint to the seeming randomness of everyday life.

An analogy might help here. When a person is inaugurated President of the United States, the event takes place in a particular ritual of prayer, the singing of the national anthem, the taking of the oath on a Bible held by the President's spouse. The ritual of inauguration, laden with American tradition, prevents the President's address from becoming just another political stump speech filled with accusations about one's opponents and the evils of the other party. While each address is, in Wainwright's word, "unrepeatable" because it offers a specific message for this particular audience, the inauguration ritual anchors the speech in the wider themes of community, reconciliation, and unity plus the traditional values of the republic. Poetic metaphors like "the torch has been passed to a new generation" or "a city on the hill" replace partisan prose. In a similar way, while the existential context of the liturgical assembly allows for a fresh and bold proclamation of the gospel, the stability of liturgical ritual guarantees a proclamation that is biblical, ecclesial, and eschatologically oriented. The stability of the liturgy helps the homily lead the assembly to prayer and a life lived in conformity with the gospel.

If the homily is "part of the liturgy itself," it follows that the same theological categories we use for Christian worship are appropriate to the homily as well. The homily is *doxological, anamnetic, epikletic, eschatological,* and *ecclesial.*[52]

a) *Doxological*

The homily is meant to give praise and thanks to God. St. Justin Martyr's *First Apology*'s description of a mid-second-century liturgy demonstrates how the presider/preacher urged and invited the assembly in such a way that it led to "prayers and thanksgivings." The patristic homilies often ended with a doxology. St. John Chrysostom believed that the closing doxology of the homily was a "proper conclusion" because the entire homily was directed to the glory of God.[53] At the beginning of the Eucharistic Prayer we say, "Let us give thanks to the Lord our God. It is right to give him thanks and praise." An indispensable criteria for an effective homily is that it animates the assembly to give God thanks and praise. *FIYH* states that "the homily points to the presence of God in people's lives and then leads a congregation into the Eucharist, providing, as it were, the motive for celebrating the Eucharist in this time and place" (23).

b) *Anamnetic*

The homily is meant to remember what God has done for us especially in Christ's paschal death and resurrection. Borrowing a term from biblical scholarship, Robert Taft reminds us: "The liturgy is the on-going *Sitz im Leben* of Christ's saving pattern in every age, and what we do in the liturgy is exactly what the New Testament itself did with Christ: it applied him and what he was and is to the present."[54]

From the beginning Christian preaching was centered on Jesus Christ, crucified and risen. A frequent theme of patristic homilies was that Christ was as present in the biblical readings as he was in the eucharistic meal. This tradition was recaptured in Vatican II's teaching of the various "presences" of Christ, e.g., "[Christ] is present in the word since it is he himself who speaks when the holy scriptures are read in the Church" (*SC*, 7). The anamnetic character of the homily was retrieved by the council when it spoke of a "proclamation of God's wonderful works in the history of salvation, which is the mystery of Christ ever made present and active in us, especially in the celebration of the liturgy" (*SC*, 35). Preserving the anamnetic character of the homily guards against Pelagian preaching which emphasizes our own deeds rather than what God has done for us.

From ancient times special attention was given to the gospel reading since it was in the proclamation of the Gospel that the faithful most keenly sensed what God had done for them in Jesus Christ. The arrangement of biblical texts in the Roman Lectionary continues this christocentric tradition of preaching. This tradition will be examined in chapter 3.

c) *Epikletic*

Just as we invoke the Holy Spirit *(epiclesis)* on the eucharistic bread and wine in the anaphora, so too do we need to invoke the Holy Spirit on our interpretation. We have pointed to the shift in *FIYH* from an interpretation of the biblical texts of the liturgy to an interpretation of the assembly's life experience in light of those texts. While the homilist makes use of the best contemporary tools of social analysis to read the signs of the times, homiletic interpretation is not merely social analysis. It is always made in the context of prayer and meditation. Homiletic preparation is not just an intellectual exercise but a spiritual exercise. Pope John Paul II believes that in the ministry of the word, serious study must be "constantly accompanied by prayer, meditation, and the invocation of the gifts of the Holy Spirit: wisdom, understanding, counsel, fortitude, knowledge, piety, and the fear of the Lord."[55]

The epikletic character of the homily challenges partisan politics, personal biases, and arrogant pronouncements about our world. Joan Delaplane is convinced that "without consciousness of the place of God's Spirit, the whole preaching endeavor for some individuals may easily become overwhelming and discouraging; for others, simply an ego trip."[56] Effective preaching requires a discernment of what specific phase of human life and what particular word from Scripture needs to be addressed. St. Paul spoke of his preaching as "not in word only, but also in power and in the Holy Spirit and with full conviction" (1 Thess 1:5).

d) *Eschatological*

The sacraments commemorate what has happened in the death and resurrection of Christ, make the paschal mystery "present and active within us," and forecast the glorious age to come. Thus, sacraments are always "signs of conversion." They remind us that the reign of God has begun but is not yet completed. In the eucharistic

Communion we find a foretaste of the messianic banquet of the kingdom. The eschatological nature of the liturgy helps us to view the homily as a proclamation of a tenacious hope for the coming of the reign of God and a call to convert to the way God wants the world to be. If the sacraments are "signs of conversion" it follows that the homily should be a sign of conversion. It should echo the prophetic preaching of Jesus who announced, "The time is fulfilled, and the kingdom of God has come near; repent, and believe in the good news" (Mark 1:15). That proclamation was a call to live in a new way, a way marked by mercy, justice, love, forgiveness, and peace-making. Liturgical preaching is both heavenly and earthly. It is the heavenly vision that gives power to the new earthly vision. On March 24, 1980, Archbishop Oscar Romero of San Salvador was shot to death as he preached a homily at Mass in the chapel of Divine Providence Hospital. His last words dramatically reflect the eschatological nature of the homily:

> This holy mass, this Eucharist, is clearly an act of faith. This body broken and blood shed for human beings encourages us to give our body and blood up to suffering and pain, as Christ did—not for self, but to bring justice and peace to our people. Let us be intimately united in faith and hope at this moment. . . .[57]

e) *Ecclesial*

The influential theologian of the Second Vatican Council Yves Congar believed that the liturgy is "the expression of a Church actively living, praising God and bringing about a holy communion with him."[58] We are most visibly Church when gathered at the table of the Lord in prayer. "Because there is one bread, we who are many are one body, for we all partake of the one bread" (1 Cor 10:17). The Church is a visible sacrament of God's saving unity: "Established by Christ as a communion of life, love and truth, it is taken up by him also as the instrument for the salvation of all; as the light of the world and the salt of the earth . . . it is sent forth into the whole world" (*LG*, 9).

Since the homily is part of the liturgy itself it can never be isolated from the great prayer of the Church. Today there is a strong proclivity to identify the sacred with the private. The ecclesial nature of the liturgy provides a healthy corrective to this "Jesus and I" spirituality and preaching. *FIYH* insists that the ecclesial characteristic of the homily provides the people with a "common vision":

Through words drawn from the Scriptures, from the church's theological tradition, and from the personal appropriation of that tradition through study and prayer, the preacher joins himself and the congregation in a common vision. We can say, therefore, that the homily is a unifying moment in the celebration of the liturgy, deepening and giving expression to the unity that is already present through the sacrament of baptism (6,7).

3) *Kerygmatic*

Vatican II's retrieval of the homily occurred during the so-called kerygmatic movement of the time which was a reaction against sermons that were more about doctrines defended than the Good News of God's saving acts boldly proclaimed. The kerygmatic character is found in the first definition of the homily given by the council: "a proclamation of God's wonderful works in the history of salvation" (*SC,* 35). In a world gloomy in its perspective and suspicious of its future, preachers are called to be what Pope John Paul II has called "heralds of hope."[59] We will treat the kerygmatic characteristic of the homily in greater depth in the next chapter when we examine the image of the preacher as herald.

4) *Conversational*

One area of thought has remained consistent in church history, the normative liturgical documents, and homiletic textbooks: preachers must speak in a manner that is accessible to their listeners. From the beginning, the Gospel was preached not in sacred languages but in the language of the people. Jesus spoke Aramaic, Paul choose *koinē* Greek. Origen chose not the stylized rhetoric of the academy but the familiar discourse of his culture. St. Francis of Assisi rejected the scholastic sermon with its endless divisions and points. He preferred the *sermo humilis* since his preaching was addressed to "the unlearned people through visible and simple things."[60] To reach the people Francis drew upon the lyrics of the popular songs of his day. His concern for the listener evolved a Franciscan preaching tradition distinguished by its simplicity, concreteness, immediacy, and affectivity.[61]

Whenever there was a new turn to the particular context of the listener, new methods of preaching evolved. In our own time a similar phenomenon can be found. The so-called New Homiletic began with a keen observation of the contemporary context of preaching.

In *As One Without Authority* (1971) Fred Craddock focused his attention on the listeners and the various methods of preaching. Craddock eschewed the traditional *deductive* method of preaching which moved from a general truth to a particular application because such an authoritarian method supposed "passive listeners who accept the right or authority of the speaker to state conclusions which he then applies to their faith and life."[62] Influenced by Gerhard Ebeling's "New Hermeneutic," Craddock highlighted the linguistic dimensions of the sermon, the importance of Jesus' parables, and the oral, experiential, and event character of preaching. He advocated an *inductive* method of preaching which begins with the particulars of human experience. This method allows listeners to dwell with the sermon and share a journey with the preacher toward the surprising conclusion of the gospel. Preaching thus becomes the shared activity of preacher and listeners.

Other homileticians such as Richard Jensen, Charles Rice, Don Wardlaw, and Eugene Lowry followed Craddock's revolution in developing "narrative preaching." These authors rebelled against sermons that were propositional rather than narrative. Since we do not live in a world shaped by points but by stories, the narrative homileticians sought to jettison the three-point sermon that was shaped like a lawyer's brief and to shape their sermons like stories.[63]

David Buttrick's homiletic begins with a systematic analysis of the role language plays in defining a culture.[64] For Buttrick language is not static or inert but a dynamic means of affecting human consciousness and shaping it. His phenomenologically-oriented homiletic deals with how language "forms" in and preaching shapes the consciousness of a congregation. Whereas homiletic manuals in the past often focused on the preacher as source, Buttrick's work is guided by "receiver-orientation." He favors a sermon method with strategically developed "moves" (not "points") from the listeners' viewpoint. We do not live our lives, dream our dreams, pray our prayers, or express our love in points. Why, then, should we preach in points?

Buttrick builds his homiletic on observing how language moves in familiar conversation:

> Most human conversation does not employ labored transitions but shifts easily, by kinds of logical association from one idea to another. About the only time we wield transitional language is when we interrupt a flowing conversation in order to turn people toward our own agendas.[65]

Recently the New Homiletic has moved its attention to the role of imagination and images in preaching. Once again, this new move is triggered by the particular context of preaching. Thomas Troeger writes that "we preachers need to build our sermons so that our listeners can step securely from image to image, from story to story, and thus climb up into the truths of their lives."[66] Employing an archetypal perspective, James Wallace calls for imaginal preaching in which the homilist does not look for a main idea or the key thought but for the dominant image in the biblical text and for "the images that we are given by life and by the faith tradition we serve."[67]

The continuing development of the New Homiletic is a contemporary attempt at a method of preaching in which the assembly recognizes that the homily is *for them and about them*. The homily is not an oration. While we may look to some of the patristic homilies as examples of familiar conversation, we are called to preach in words and images that are familiar to the faithful today. Also, we must be sensitive to the attention span of today's listeners. Jesus called his disciples "friends." His preaching was gladly heard by the common people not because of his oratorical skills but because he knew how to interpret their lives (Mark 12:37). We speak to our friends not through orations or lengthy lessons but through conversation.

The Directory on the Ministry and Life of Priests states that preachers will be effective and credible when they are "familiar with the ideology, language, cultural intricacies and the typologies diffused in the mass media."[68] *FIYH* insists that the homily will fulfill its goals "more effectively if the language it uses is specific, graphic, and imaginative" (25).

5) *Prophetic*

Thomas K. Carroll reminds us that in ancient days the "Greek word homily *(homilia)* had a social connotation and meant primarily a being together or a communion."[69] The patristic homilies proclaimed the saving grace of Jesus Christ in the midst of existential realities. The purpose of preaching in the early Church was the salvation of the listeners. The homily sought to induce a response to the demands of the Good News.[70] Even the patristic preaching that initiated candidates into the Christian mysteries reveled in comparisons and contrasts between elements of human culture and the events of the initiation process. The prophetic aspect is especially highlighted in

FIYH where the homily is described not as an interpretation of the Bible nor an explanation of a doctrine or theme. The homily is an interpretation of life in light of the Good News.

Homilists must always search for the key connection between the liturgical celebration and the cultural context. Do we come to liturgy as we do a filling station to "tank up" with God's grace so that we can make it in the culture in which we live? If that is our notion, we will be tempted to view the liturgical preaching as a tool to apply biblical themes, church teachings, or social action to our lives. John Baldovin challenges this liturgical perspective where liturgists and preachers think that they are the experts whose "task is to instruct the assembly about some worthy theme with the result that the assembly itself is alienated."[71]

An alternative to the "filling station" notion of the liturgical assembly is the liturgical thought of Karl Rahner. He argued that the "first" or "primary" liturgy that a church assembly celebrates is what he called the "Liturgy of the World." Rahner believed that the world itself is always and everywhere grasped at its roots by God's self-communication of grace. The sacraments are "small signs" of the fact that this entire world belongs to God. Rahner's liturgical theology is rooted in the Catholic sacramental tradition which believes that we can encounter God by encountering the human. He challenged the conventional view of liturgy as the means through which grace is made available to a world that is ordinarily deprived of it. Rahner believed that our celebration of the Church's liturgy explicitly expresses the limitlessness of God's grace underlying our lives.[72]

Rahner's understanding of how the liturgy can transform our lives resonates with *FIYH*'s understanding of the homily not as an application of scriptural insights or church teaching to life but a scriptural interpretation of life within the praise and prayer of the liturgical assembly. Such a definition preserves the prophetic characteristic of the homily.

The history of preaching points to the many forces that robbed the homily of its prophetic quality: the reading of the sermons of "experts" from the past; dogmatism and moralism; preference for the Liturgy of the Eucharist over the Liturgy of the Word; lack of an integrated theology of proclamation; the loss of spiritual vision. The lessons of history are a reminder for us to detect and resist similar forces in our time that threaten the prophetic characteristic of the homily.

Besides offering an explication of the characteristics of the homily, I have also attempted to highlight in this chapter the significance of the shift in an understanding of the homily from an instructional to an interpretive act as found in *FIYH*. I will refer to these characteristics and the interpretive shift throughout the remainder of the book as we continue to explore what the homily is and what it is supposed to do.

Notes

1. William Shakespeare, *As You Like It,* act 2, scene 1.
2. Ibid., act 3, scene 2.
3. Thus, in his "Sermon" David L. Bartlett defines a sermon as "an oral interpretation of scripture, usually in the context of worship," in William Willimon and Richard Lischer, eds., *Concise Encyclopedia of Preaching* (Louisville: Westminster John Knox Press, 1995) 433.
4. See Richard A. Jensen's remarks in *Telling the Story* (Minneapolis: Augsburg, 1980) 86.
5. Henry Grady Davis, *Design for Preaching* (Philadelphia: Fortress Press, 1958) 162.
6. Donald Wilson Stake, *The ABC's of Worship: A Concise Dictionary* (Louisville: Westminster/John Knox Press, 1992) 93.
7. Charles L. Rice, *The Embodied Word: Preaching as Art and Liturgy* (Minneapolis: Fortress Press, 1991) 86.
8. Ibid., 86–7.
9. Justin Martyr, The First Apology, chapter 67, *Writings of Saint Justin Martyr,* trans. Thomas B. Falls (New York: Christian Heritage, 1948) 106–7.
10. Oscar Cullmann, *Vatican II. The New Direction* (New York: Harper and Row, 1968) 99.
11. See Thomas K. Carroll, *Preaching the Word, Message of the Fathers of the Church,* vol. 11 (Wilmington: Michael Glazier, 1984) 43.
12. Joseph T. Lienhard, S.J., "Origen As Homilist," *Preaching in the Patristic Age: Studies in Honor of Walter J. Burghardt, S.J.,* ed. David G. Hunter (New York: Paulist Press, 1989) 45.
13. Ibid., 36.
14. Carroll, *Preaching the Word,* 43.
15. Homily on Leviticus 1.4, *The Fathers of the Church: Origen: Homilies of Leviticus 1–6,* trans. Gary Wayne Barkley, vol. 83 (Washington, D.C.: Catholic University of America Press, 1990) 35.
16. Saint Augustine, bishop (*Sermo 304,* 1–4: PL 38, 1395–1397) trans. of International Committee on English in the Liturgy, Inc. as found in *The Liturgy of the Hours* (New York: Catholic Book Publishing, 1975) 1306.

17. Yngve Brilioth, *A Brief History of Preaching,* trans. Karl E. Mattson (Philadelphia: Fortress Press, 1965) 67.

18. Ibid., 89.

19. See J. Kevin Coyle, "From Homily to Sermon to Homily: The Content of Christian Preaching in Historical Perspective," *Liturgical Ministry* (Winter 1992) 7.

20. Brilioth, *A Brief History of Preaching,* 73.

21. As reported by Frederick J. McGinness, *Right Thinking and Sacred Oratory in Counter-Reformation Rome* (Princeton, N.J.: Princeton University Press, 1995) 34.

22. *Canons and Decrees of Trent,* trans. H. J. Schroeder, S.J. (St. Louis: B. Herder Book Co., 1941) 26.

23. *St. Francis of Assisi: His Life and Writings as Recorded by His Contemporaries,* trans. Leo Sherley-Price (London: A. R. Mowbray, 1959) 232–3.

24. St. Augustine, *On Christian Doctrine,* trans. D. W. Robertson, Jr. (New York: Liberal Arts Press, 1978) 4.25.55, 141.

25. McGinness, *Right Thinking and Sacred Oratory,* 33.

26. Ibid., 55.

27. Thomas V. Liske, *Effective Preaching* (New York: MacMillan, 1960) 149.

28. As quoted in *Vatican II: An Interfaith Appraisal,* John H. Miller, C.S.C., ed. (Notre Dame, Ind.: University of Notre Dame Press, 1966) 29.

29. Gerard S. Sloyan, "Preaching at Mass," in *North American Liturgical Week Proceedings, 1963* (Washington, D.C.: Liturgical Conference, 1964) 193.

30. William Skudlarek, O.S.B., *The Word in Worship: Preaching in a Liturgical Context* (Nashville: Abingdon Press, 1981) 82.

31. Ibid., 93.

32. O.C. Edwards, Jr., *Elements of Homiletic: A Method for Preparing to Preach* (New York: Pueblo Publishing, 1982; Collegeville: The Liturgical Press, 1990) 6–7.

33. John Broadus, *A Treatise on the Preparation and Delivery of Sermons* (New York: A.C. Armstrong & Son, 1889) 31.

34. Joseph Gelineau, *The Liturgy Today and Tomorrow* (New York: Paulist Press, 1978) 81.

35. See the description of preaching at Kaddish by Ismar Elbogen, *Jewish Liturgy: A Comprehensive History* (Philadelphia: The Jewish Publication Society, 1993) 80. We ordinarily think of Kaddish as a mourner's prayer for the departed, but the ancient Kaddish was not known for this until the thirteenth century. See Ralph Posner and Uri Kaploun and Shalom Cohen, eds., *Jewish Liturgy* (New York: Leon Amiel Publisher, 1975) 112: "Primarily it (Kaddish) is characterized by abundance of Messianic hope for the speedy establishment of God's kingdom on earth."

36. Gerard S. Sloyan, "Is Church Teaching Neglected When the Lectionary Is Preached?" *Worship* (March 1987) 131.

37. Kevin W. Irwin, *Context and Text: Method in Liturgical Theology* (Collegeville: The Liturgical Press, 1994) 91.

38. Ibid., 106–7.

39. The Bishops' Committee on Priestly Life and Ministry, National Conference of Catholic Bishops, *Fulfilled in Your Hearing: The Homily in The Sunday Assembly* (Washington, D.C.: United States Catholic Conference, 1982) 17.

40. Dennis C. Smolarski, S.J., *Liturgical Literary: From Anamnesis to Worship* (New York: Paulist Press, 1990) 124.

41. Edwards, *Elements of Homiletic,* 13.

42. Paul Bradshaw, "Liturgical Use and Abuse of Patristics," *Liturgy Reshaped,* ed. Kenneth Stevenson (London: SPCK, 1982) 144.

43. Mary Collins, O.S.B., "Liturgical Homily: Connecting the Body," *Eucharist: Toward the Third Millennium,* ed. Gerard Austin (Chicago: Liturgy Training Publications, 1997) 94.

44. Geoffrey Wainwright, "Preaching as Worship" *The Greek Orthodox Theological Review* (Winter 1983) 331.

45. The Pontifical Biblical Commission, *The Interpretation of the Bible in the Church* (Rome: Libreria Editrice Vaticana, 1993) 34.

46. Ibid., 31.

47. Ibid., 117.

48. Heribert B. Joné, *Moral Theology,* ed. and trans. Urban Adelman (Westminster, Md.: Newman Press, 1958) 123: "*Venial sin* is committed by voluntarily omitting an unimportant part of the Mass, e.g., from the beginning of the Mass to the Offertory exclusive, or the part that follows the Communion, or even the part which precedes the Epistle together with that which follows the Communion."

49. Irwin, *Context and Text,* 5.

50. Geoffrey Wainwright, "The Sermon and the Liturgy," *The Greek Orthodox Theological Review* (Winter 1983) 346.

51. See Victor Turner, *The Ritual Process* (Chicago: Adine Publication Company, 1969) and Ronald Grimes, *Beginnings in Ritual Studies* (Washington, D.C.: University of America Press, 1982).

52. The view of Geoffrey Wainwright, "Preaching As Worship," 326. Wainwright used the four characteristics, doxological, anamnetic, epikletic, and eschatological to describe the liturgical nature of preaching. Because the Church is most Church when gathered at Eucharist, I have added ecclesial as a fifth characteristic.

53. *Homily 16:10 on Letter to the Romans.*

54. Robert Taft, S.J., *The Liturgy of the Hours in East and West* (Collegeville: The Liturgical Press, 1986) 336.

55. Pope John Paul II, *Gift and Mystery: On the Fiftieth Anniversary of My Priestly Ordination* (New York: Doubleday 1996) 92.

56. Joan Delaplane, O.P., "The Living Word: An Overshadowing of the Spirit," Aquinas Institute of Theology Faculty, *In the Company of Preachers* (Collegeville: The Liturgical Press, 1993) 141.

57. Oscar Romero, *A Martyr's Message of Hope* (Kansas City, Mo.: Celebration Books, 1983) 166.

58. Yves Congar, O.P., *Tradition and Traditions,* trans. Michael Naseby and Thomas Rainborough (New York: Macmillan, 1966) 427.

59. John Paul II, "Inaugural Address to the IV General Conference of Latin American Bishops" (Santo Domingo, October 12–28, 1992) n.24: *AAS* (1993) 827.

60. Thomas of Celano, *The Second Life of St. Francis,* LXXIII, 107 in *St. Francis of Assisi: Writings and Early Biographies,* ed. Marion A. Habig (Chicago: Franciscan Herald Press, 1973) 450.

61. See Michael W. Blastic, O.F.M., Conv., "Franciscans," *Concise Encyclopedia of Preaching,* 158–160.

62. Fred B. Craddock, *As One Without Authority* (Nashville: Abingdon Press, 1971) 54.

63. Richard A. Jensen, *Telling the Story* (Minneapolis: Augsburg, 1980); Eugene L. Lowry, *The Homiletic Plot* (Atlanta: John Knox, 1980); Edmund Steimele, Morris Neidenthal and Charles Rice, *Preaching the Story* (Philadelphia: Fortress Press, 1980); Don M. Wardlaw, *Preaching Biblically: Creating Sermons in the Shape of Scripture* (Philadelphia: Fortress Press, 1983); Robert P. Waznak, S.S., *Sunday After Sunday: Preaching the Homily as Story* (New York: Paulist Press, 1983).

64. David Buttrick, *Homiletic: Moves and Structures* (Philadelphia: Fortress Press, 1987).

65. Ibid., 70

66. Thomas Troeger, *Creating Fresh Images for Preaching* (Valley Forge: Judson, 1982) 30.

67. James A. Wallace, C.Ss.R., *Imaginal Preaching: An Archetypal Perspective* (New York: Paulist Press, 1995) 18.

68. Congregation for the Clergy, *Directory on the Ministry and Life of Priests* (Citta Del Vaticano: Libreria Editrice Vaticana, 1994) 48.

69. Carroll, *Preaching the Word,* 18.

70. See P.T. Weller, *Selected Easter Sermons of St. Augustine* (St. Louis: Herder, 1959) 3–59.

71. John F. Baldovin, S.J., "The Nature and Function of the Liturgical Homily," *The Way: Supplement 67* (1990) 94.

72. For a fine review of Karl Rahner's thoughts on the "Liturgy of the World," see Michael Skelley, S.J., *The Liturgy of the World: Karl Rahner's Theology of Worship* (Collegeville: The Liturgical Press, 1991).

2

The Homilist as Herald, Teacher, Interpreter, and Witness

Avery Dulles began his influential book *Models of the Church* with the thesis that the Church, like other theological realities, is a mystery and "in order to do justice to the various aspects of the Church, as a complex reality, we must work simultaneously with different models."[1] From Roman Catholic ecclesiology Dulles presented five models of the Church and assessed their respective strengths and weaknesses.

In a similar way, when we focus on the homilist, we begin to discover a complexity of images. Prominent homiletician Thomas G. Long claims that when preachers go to the pulpit they carry certain controlling images of themselves as ministers. Consciously or unconsciously, preachers see themselves as "shepherds" or "prophets" or "enablers" or "evangelists" or "wounded healers." Long believes that when a preacher delivers a sermon, "that act is embedded in some larger framework of ministerial self-understanding."[2] He identifies three "master" metaphors or controlling images from contemporary homiletic scholarship: the *herald,* the *pastor,* and the *storyteller.* Long adds to this list the image which he believes is more suited than any of the others to disclose the true character of Christian preaching: the *witness.*

The image of *herald* was popular in Catholic liturgical literature at the time of the Second Vatican Council when the homily was described as a "proclamation of God's wonderful works in the history of salvation" (*SC,* 35). Proclaiming is the work of heralds. In chapter 1 we saw how the image of *teacher* was emphasized in the Roman

Catholic tradition, especially from the period of Trent to Vatican II. We also found a new image of the homilist in *Fulfilled in Your Hearing*: "mediator of meaning" or interpreter of God's word and world. I prefer to view the homiletic metaphors of pastor, storyteller, and prophet (poet) under the master image of *interpreter*. The image of the preacher as *witness* has not been prominent in normative liturgical documents but does appear in other church texts. This image is significant, especially in our times which place a high premium on the credibility and personality of the preacher. If Thomas Long is correct, and I believe he is, then how one preaches the homily depends to a large degree on how one views oneself as either *herald, teacher, interpreter,* or *witness.* What follows is a review of homiletic thought and debate concerning these four master images that have influenced and continue to influence the Catholic preaching tradition, plus an assessment of their strengths and weaknesses.[3]

The Herald[4]

The word most frequently used for preaching in the New Testament is *kērussein* (proclaim). The preacher is like the herald *(kērux)* whose task is to announce a message from the monarch. John the Baptist cries out in the desert as a messianic herald. Jesus, and those who followed him, proclaim the impending reign of God. What matters is not the style or form of the message or the personality of the herald. What matters is the message. It is the responsibility of the herald to pass it on unchanged from monarch to people. St. Paul declared: "My speech and my proclamation were not with plausible words of wisdom, but with a demonstration of the Spirit and of power" (1 Cor 2:4). Such preaching is found in the apostolic preaching of Acts: 2:14-40; 3:12-26; 10:28-43. In ancient days, before the herald proclaimed a message, there was a flourish of trumpets to compel the attention of the citizens, and a display of credentials. In a similar way the New Testament herald is the very mouthpiece of God whose preaching compels those who hear it with the necessity of a response: "So we are ambassadors of Christ, since God is making his appeal through us; we entreat you on behalf of Christ, be reconciled to God" (2 Cor 5:20).

Another important New Testament word for preaching is *euaggelizein* (to proclaim the Good News). The preacher is like the *euaggelistes* (bringer of Good News) who in ancient Greek times rode ahead of the troops to the people who anxiously awaited the news of the battle. Wearing a garland around his head, he would raise his hand and cry out the good news in a loud voice: "Greetings, we have won!" The apostolic preaching was about the Good News that Christ had won the battle by his cross and resurrection.

The Second Vatican Council insisted that a kerygmatic character permeate the homily. It emphasized "the proclamation of God's wonderful works in the history of salvation, which is the mystery of Christ ever made present and active in us, especially in the celebration of the liturgy" (*SC*, 35). This statement was influenced by the so-called kerygmatic movement at the time. That movement arose in the mid- and late-thirties when some Catholic theologians were rethinking and writing about the nature and method of theology. For these scholars theology had drifted from its biblical base because of an intellectualist-conceptualist search for *truth*. The Austrian theologian Josef Jungmann (1889–1975) was the father of the kerygmatic movement that emphasized the proclamation of the Good News. Kerygmatic preaching and teaching focused on the *kērygma* or the core of the gospel first preached by the apostles: the saving acts of God in Christ. Jungmann deplored the preaching of his day which he said was no more than a "vulgarization of theological tracts." His oft-repeated question was "Do we really preach the gospel?" In 1936 he published a small volume, *Die Frohbotschaft und unsere Glaubensverkündigung* (The Good News and Our Proclamation of the Faith), in which he pleaded for a total and christocentric kerygma in the Church where Christianity is first of all a fact and only secondarily a doctrine. The book's "novel" concepts aroused controversy and so it was withdrawn from circulation for fear of incurring ecclesiastical censure. It was not translated and edited into English until 1962.[5] Jungmann claimed that Catholics were devoid of joy and enthusiasm in the life of faith because of the exaggerated intellectualism of scientific theology. Instead of hearing the Good News of their redemption in Christ, all they heard from pulpits were dogmatic and moral precepts, dos and don'ts, threats and promises, customs and rites. Just after Vatican II had finished its first session, Jungmann produced a second book entitled *Glaubensverkündigung im Lichte der Frohbotschaft* (1963), bearing the English title *Announcing the Word of God* (1967), in which he insisted that the content of preaching be "what Christ himself proclaimed and what his apostles proclaimed abroad as heralds: that the kingdom of God had entered the world, thus disclosing salvation to mankind [sic]."[6]

An example of the influence of the kerygmatic movement on preaching in the United States in the early 1960s is found in an article by William O'Shea:

> Preaching, as the first Christians understood it, was not merely a religious discourse, nor was it a kind of catechetical instruction as you might hear in a classroom. It was, above all, a heralding, a proclamation of the Kingdom that had come . . . There is a note of "news" about it; it is a tidings, something to be cried aloud. It is not a proposition to be explained or defended; it is a communication from a sovereign . . . The Christian preacher is not a professor, nor again is he a propagandist. He is a herald with something to communicate, and that something is the Gospel–God's Gospel–God's plan of salvation.[7]

The term "kerygmatic" is not as fashionable as it was during the time of Vatican II. Some wonder if it was merely a fly-by-night scheme to help attack the "vulgarization of theological tracts" prevalent in Roman Catholic pulpits. There is little mention of it in contemporary theological dictionaries and encyclopedias. Karl Rahner devotes only a small paragraph to kerygmatic theology in the *Lexikon für Theologie und Kirche.*[8]

Although "kerygmatic" is no longer popular in Catholic theological discourse, it nevertheless offers a significant benchmark for defining the character that should permeate the homily. Pope John Paul II frequently urges the need for "heralds of hope" in what he calls "the new evangelization." There are three compelling reasons to preserve the herald image restored at the time of Vatican II: It *(1) focuses on the gospel rather than on "more important" topics; (2) challenges narcissistic preaching; (3) offers a needed word of encouragement in a world desperately searching for meaning.*

1) *Focuses on the gospel rather than on "more important" topics*

A great cry of the Reformers was that priests were preaching everything *but* the Word of God. This is how Martin Luther described the preaching of his day:

> After the text of the Gospels is read, they take us to fairyland. One preaches from Aristotle and the heathen books, another from the papal decretals. One brings questions about his holy Order, another about blue ducks, another about hen's milk . . . In short, this is the art in which nobody sticks to the text, from which people might have had the gospel.[9]

Church historian, Robert F. McNamara, carefully examined American Roman Catholic preaching legislation from 1791–1975.[10] He catalogued a remarkable list of rules from plenary councils and diocesan synods in which bishops warned their priests not to preach arbitrary moral laws, advocate particular political candidates, complain about their inadequate salaries, voice personal grievances, use as illustrations "old wives' tales" that might cause Protestants to laugh and Catholics to squirm.[11] The fact that such legislation was deemed necessary by the bishops demonstrates that such non-kerygmatic preaching did take place in Catholic pulpits. Preserving the kerygmatic mark of the homily reminds us that the Second Vatican Council declared that the homily "is the proclamation of God's wonderful works in the history of salvation, which is the mystery of Christ ever made present and active in us, especially in the celebration of the liturgy" (*SC,* 35).

2) *Challenges narcissistic preaching*

The herald image stresses that the preacher is a minister who preaches from the Bible as the Church's book. The herald image challenges the preacher who is narcissistic, is ignorant of the Church's tradition, and is concerned more with pop psychology, home spun advice, and the power of positive thinking than the proclamation of the Good News. Quoting from Pope John Paul II, the 1994 *Directory on the Ministry and Life of Priests* states that the role of the preacher "is not to teach his own wisdom, but the Word of God and to issue an urgent invitation to all men [sic] to conversion and to holiness."[12]

The herald image preserves the ancient homiletic advice that we are to preach not ourselves but Christ. That tradition is found in St. Paul who cautioned those who preached merely their own thing: "For I want you to know, brothers and sisters, that the gospel that was proclaimed by me is not of human origin; for I did not receive it from a human source, nor was I taught it, but I received it through a revelation of Jesus Christ" (Gal 1:11-13).

3) *Offers a needed word of encouragement in a world desperately searching for meaning*

FIYH highlights kerygmatic preaching when it states: "Although we have received this good news, believed in it and sealed our faith in the sacrament of baptism, we need to rediscover the truth of it again and again in our lives" (19). The restored homily of Vatican II was meant to give listeners a word that would enable them to celebrate Eucharist, to give praise and thanks to God. We do not proclaim the Good News in a glass cathedral where the sun shines so brightly that the cross and all other symbols of mystery and finitude are effectively eclipsed. Edward Schillebeeckx contends that God is encountered not directly but rather "on the underside" or "in contrast."[13] Commenting on Schillebeeckx's theology of revelation, Mary Catherine Hilkert writes: "God is present to the majority of the world's population in the way God was present to Jesus in the crucifixion—as a source of endurance and hope in the darkness and apparent abandonment and as a promise to be the faithful 'God of the Living'. . . ."[14]

The proclamation of the Good News does not mean, therefore, that the preacher ignores the demons in our midst. William A. Richard has cautioned against preaching the Good News without hearing the bad news. By bad news Richard speaks in broad categories of "the expectation of the seeming absence of God" and "the recognition of our human inadequacy, or worse, our sinfulness."[15] We celebrate Eucharist in memory of Jesus Christ who *on the night before he died* turned to God and praised and thanked God in his hour of distress. We celebrate Eucharist in the context of a world filled with bad news: the fear of crime driven by a drug-infested culture; old racial and religious hatreds and economic injustices that still threaten world peace and stability; the vulnerability we share because of overpopulation, the spread of AIDS, and the nuclear and environmental crises; the tragic events that penetrate the lives of ordinary people who come to liturgy each week, like the death of a child or the loss of employment and health benefits. Contemporary sociologists have called religion a meaning system. How does the preacher bring meaning to people whose lives are sometimes dull, chaotic, and threatening? Pop psychology, homiletic bromides, and the power of positive thinking are not the answers. What frees people from the slavery of our times is not a proclamation of gloom but the Good News.

The proclamation of the Good News does not mean that a prophetic voice is not heard. The Good News proclaimed by the angels and by Simeon and Anna in the temple about the birth of "a Savior who is Christ the Lord" comes with a solemn warning: "This child is destined for the falling and the rising of many in Israel, to be a sign that will be opposed so that the inner thoughts of many will be revealed" (Luke 2:34). Raymond Brown has written that "the gospel is always a factor that produces judgment; and the joy of the 'good news' has also an element of sadness because not all will believe."[16]

The herald preacher dares to proclaim the Good News without ignoring the bad news of our lives nor muting the call to conversion and a turning away from sin. *FIYH* tells us that we cannot proclaim the Good News without first recognizing the active presence of God in our own lives, broken and shattered as they may be:

> We can and must praise God even when we do not feel like it, for praise and thanksgiving are rooted in and grow out of faith, not feeling, a faith which interprets this world by saying that in spite of appearances to the contrary, our God is a loving God . . . The challenge to preachers then is to reflect on human life with the aid of the Word of God and to show by their preaching as by their lives, that in every place and at every time it is indeed right to praise and thank the Lord (27–8).

Before we leave this reflection on the herald image in Catholic preaching we should also consider some of its shortcomings and accompanying caveats. The herald image *(1) tends to obscure the context of preaching; (2) tends to discourage serious homiletic preparation; (3) cannot be neatly isolated from teaching.*

1) *Tends to obscure the context of preaching*

The timeless nature of the herald's message might ignore the importance of a message that needs to be proclaimed in a particular time with particular concerns. That is the reason we have four Gospels. The evangelists proclaimed the same timeless message about Christ's death and resurrection but proclaimed it to the particular needs of their listeners. They proclaimed to the people: "This Good News is for us!"

Preaching never takes place in a vacuum. It takes place in a particular context with its own concerns, dreams, and problems. It is preached not by some disembodied individual but by a live flesh and blood preacher with a unique personality. The bishops of Vatican II were sensitive to the context of preaching when they insisted that "preaching must not present God's Word in a general and abstract fashion only, but it must apply the perennial truth of the Gospel to the concrete circumstances of life" (*PO,* 4). In his apostolic exhortation

On Evangelization in the Modern World, Pope Paul VI wrote: "This is why evangelization involves an explicit message adapted to the different situations constantly being realized, about the rights and duties of every human being, about family life . . . about international life, peace, justice and liberation—a message especially energetic about liberation."[17]

2) *Tends to discourage serious homiletic preparation*

The herald image with its highly transcendent stamp could lead preachers to believe that all they have to do is open their mouths since they are God's mouthpieces. The image could be misused by passive preachers who think their priestly ordination alone guarantees their right to preaching without concern for preparation, for choosing the most effective words and style in order to reach their listeners. Walter Burghardt has offered thousands of American preachers a healthy sense of guilt by telling them that for every minute of his homilies, he spends four hours of preparation. For Burghardt, "the unprepared homilist is a menace. I do not minimize divine inspiration; I simply suggest it is rarely allotted to the lazy."[18] John Paul II believes "much attention must be given to the homily . . . it should always be carefully prepared, rich in substance, and adapted to the hearers."[19]

Many of the great preachers of the patristic era, such as Augustine, John Chrysostom, and the Cappadocians had pursued careers as rhetors before beginning to preach. They did not throw out the rhetorical baby with the bath water but utilized the principles of classical rhetoric in their preaching. Aristotle had defined rhetoric as using "all of the available means of persuasion." Augustine's Book IV of his *De Doctrina Christiana* borrowed classical rhetorical principles to help the preachers of his day to become more persuasive in their sermons. In our own day, the term "rhetoric" conjures up the deceitful speech of politicians or the slick advertising techniques of Madison Avenue. "That's mere rhetoric!" we say. This was not how Augustine viewed rhetoric. He saw it as a necessary science that enabled preachers and teachers to present the truth in an effective manner. Augustine writes:

> If anyone says, however, that if teachers are made learned by the Holy Spirit they do not need to be taught by men what they should say or how they should say it, he should also say that we should not pray because the Lord says, "for your Father knoweth what is needful for you, before you ask him."[20]

The herald image has the potential of misuse by preachers who are concerned neither with job security nor effectiveness. Catholic priests were never under the same pressures of homiletic profession-alism as many Protestant preachers whose job security depended on an ability to preach effectively. The herald image could provide jus-tification for those content to rest on their presbyteral status rather than the serious study and prayerful imagination required of effec-tive homilists.

3) *Cannot be neatly isolated from teaching*

Joseph Fichtner speculates that the reason kerygmatic theology re-ceived such short shrift from Catholic theologians was because "of its pretention to be a distinct and independent theology." Fichtner takes a balanced position when he writes that kerygmatic theology should "serve a function complementary to and within scientific theology." He cautions that "it was not meant to be used as a pretext for an anti-intellectual and pseudo-pastoral attitude which would ill prepare can-didates for the ministry of the word."[21]

Preaching is a theological task. It was so from the beginning of Christianity. The *kērygma* found in the New Testament manifests the-ologizing. The synoptics reflect a theological interpretation of the original message. Pauline and Johannine theologies continue the de-velopment of the Good News. Homilies that lack theological depth are outside the tradition of the early proclamation of the gospel. Wal-ter Burghardt observes:

> Our basic Christian words, the words we preach, must be con-stantly recaptured, rethought: God, Christ, and Spirit, sin and re-demption; church and sacraments; justice and love; death and resurrection . . . [U]ntil the clergy can read theology with under-standing and a critical eye, liturgical homiletics will continue to be impoverished.[22]

C. H. Dodd, in *The Apostolic Preaching*, made a distinction between *kērygma*, the public proclamation of the gospel, and *didachē*, the teach-ing which includes the elucidation of the truths declared in the *kērygma*.[23] Although the proclamation of the *kērygma* came first in the course of Christian preaching and *didachē* second, in truth, they were not always so easily distinguishable. Joseph Fichtner observes: "Teaching occa-sionally overlapped with proclamation in content, and the gospel was both proclaimed and taught to Christians and non-Christians."[24] The image of the herald preacher does not stand alone. The image of teacher is also part of our homiletic heritage.

The Teacher

Jesus was a teacher. He acted and was regarded by others as a teacher. Teacher or rabbi was the title given him more frequently in the New Testament than any other. The crowd was amazed at the boy Jesus in the Temple because he was in effect teaching the teachers (Luke 2:46-47). Luke emphasized the teaching ministry of Jesus at the climax of his ministry. Jesus responds to the questions put to him by the leaders of the Temple in chapters 19 and 20, and this activity Luke calls "teaching in the Temple." This teaching ministry is continued by Jesus' prophetic successors in Acts (4:2; 5:21, 25).

In the New Testament proclamation is often joined with teaching (Matt 4:23; 9:35; 11:1; Acts 28:31). Teaching is intimately connected with preaching because what the preacher declares often calls for explanation. Accounts of early Christian sermons are filled with didactic material. Paul's reported sermon at Athens in Acts makes use of theological and philosophical discussion–teaching. Some scholars have suggested that the household codes found in Pauline letters (Rom 12:12; Eph 4:17-6:9; Col 3:5-25) may be signs of an early instruction for catechumens, emphasizing the virtuous life lived in Jesus Christ. The technical word for teaching in the New Testament is *didaskein*. It is used nearly a hundred times and means to instruct by means of discourse with others.

Another word for teaching in the New Testament is catechesis *(katechein)* which comes from the Greek verb meaning "to resound, to echo." In the course of the first five centuries of the Church's history, catechesis came to be applied to the instruction given within the catechumenate to those preparing for baptism (baptismal catechesis) and to those recently baptized (mystagogical catechesis). In the early Church, Lent was a time for catechetical preaching, preparing converts for their baptism at Easter liturgy. The taproot of catechesis in the early Church was the liturgy and its method was preaching. The content of catechetical preaching was the kerygma, the paschal mystery, and the promise of God in Christ. Catechetical preaching "aimed at the intellect and heart of the convert, helping him or her know Christ better through more or less systematic instruction."[25]

The golden age of the catechumenate extended roughly from the third to the fifth century. Lawrence E. Mick cites three historical pressures which led to a formalization of the initiation process: (1) the need to reinterpret the Jesus tradition in a variety of new missionary contexts; (2) the need to standardize Christian teaching and to strengthen the catechesis since new Christians had to be well-formed in Christian beliefs because of competition from pagan philosophies, heretical movements, and the mystery religions; (3) the need to probe potential candidates more carefully. At the end of three years, the lives of the catechumens were examined, and if they were found to be ready, they were "elected" or chosen to receive the sacraments at Easter.[26]

Mystagogical catechesis was designed to explain to the newly baptized the spiritual and theological significance of the signs, symbols, and the gestures of the initiation rites that they had experienced at the Easter Vigil. Some scholars have suggested that mystagogical catechesis was adopted from the Greek and Roman mystery religions where the candidate witnessed a representation of episodes in the life of a god or goddess, and took part in the action.[27]

Mystagogical catechesis became a virtual art by the fourth century. Its practical function was to articulate the meaning of the sacraments to the newly baptized so that they could enter more fully in faith and understanding into the worship of the community. Some of the richest sources of sacramental theology are found in the mystagogical homilies of Cyril of Jerusalem, Theodore of Mopsuestia, Ambrose, John Chrysostom, and Augustine. These homilists often preached extemporaneously. Their homilies contained both a commentary upon the various symbols of the rites and a scriptural exegesis. For example, Cyril of Jerusalem explained the symbolism of the water font by referring to the waters of creation, the Exodus and the passage through the Red Sea, allusions to Second Kings and Song of Songs, plus the Lord's baptism as a precursor of his resurrection from the dead, his descent into the "nether world" and ascension into heaven.

It is important here to stress that patristic mystagogical catechesis was intimately connected with the liturgy. It was not the formal instruction of a classroom but the catechesis that naturally emerged from the proclamation of the *kērygma*, the mysteries celebrated in the liturgy, and the practical needs of the newly baptized. Enrico Mazza observes:

> The mystagogical homilies of these men are themselves liturgical
> entities, not only because they are homilies, but also and above all

because of their purpose, which is to explain to the neophytes, or newly baptized, the meaning and the nature of the liturgical actions in which they have participated: baptism and the Eucharist.[28]

The pedagogical catechesis during the preceding periods of inquiry, catechumenate, and election was not the same as mystagogical catechesis of the newly baptized. Baptism catechesis was concerned with the central truths of the early Christian faith: creation, sin, and redemption while mystagogical catechesis focused on the meaning and nature of liturgical actions.

With the widespread practice of infant baptism, the catechumenate gradually disappeared. Classroom-type instruction and catechisms took the place of baptismal and mystagogical catechesis in liturgical homilies. This does not meant that the sermons of the Middle Ages did not contain a didactic tone but it was dramatically different from the catechetical preaching of the first five centuries of the Church. Homiletic manuals, books of sermon outlines, and collections of moral tales provided preachers with expert advice on how to preach. The homiletic manuals presented the scholastic method. A sermon began with a scriptural quotation, a statement of the theme of the sermon, and a prayer. This was followed by a restatement of the theme in the introduction and a division of the argument, usually into three parts. In *The Art of Preaching,* Cistercian scholar Alan of Lille (c. 1128–1202) states that preaching "derives from the path of reason and from the fountainhead of the 'authorities.'"[29] The authorities were passages from Scripture, often backed up by other statements from patristic preachers and classic pagan verses.

The scholastic sermon which sought to prove church teaching and refute heresies was not the only kind of preaching that emerged in the Middle Ages. Dom Gregory Dix characterizes most of the preaching of the Middle Ages as moral exhortation rather than clear instruction in the teachings of the Church:

> There are attempts to arouse the people's emotions by descriptions of the passion and various other incidents of the life of our Lord like the nativity, some of which are very moving. But always the end is to move the *will* to goodness, to moral endeavour.[30]

As was noted in the last chapter, the Counter-Reformation's renewal of preaching did not restore the liturgical homily of the early Church. The Council of Trent failed to offer a coherent theology of proclamation. "[I]t was not long before Catholic (and, for that matter, Protestant) views on preaching were stressing 'orthodoxy' in distinctly polemical tones, and were once again focusing on moral exhortation and generally reviving the ills deplored by Lateran V."[31]

Chapter 1 spoke of the two schools of thought among the bishops of Vatican II. The one that favored a return to the biblical/liturgical homily of the early Church won out over the school that advocated catechetical instruction. But at the end of this century, there is a call in some circles for a return to a more instructional type of preaching.[32] There are three reasons for this call.

First, there is the shift toward a catechetical understanding of the homily found in Pope John Paul II's *Catechesi tradendae* (Apostolic Exhortation on Catechesis in Our Time) which was promulgated in 1979.[33] John Paul II agrees with the description of the homily found in Paul VI's 1975 *Evangelii nuntiandi* (Apostolic Exhortation on Evangelization in the Modern World): the homily should be liturgical, biblical, and accommodated to the listeners. But where Paul VI described the evangelical fruits of the homily as faith, hope, love, peace, and unity,[34] John Paul II hopes for catechetical fruits: familiarization with the whole of the mysteries of faith and the norms of Christian living.[35] Second, there are the fears of what some church leaders have called a "hollowing out" or "thinning" of Catholicism. They reason that Mass time is the only time to reach most of the people with church teaching. The third reason for a return to the instructional sermon is the publication of the *Catechism of the Catholic Church.* Just as the *Roman Catechism* was a homiletic guide for generations of Catholic preachers, some have seen the new catechism as providing the same potential.

The *Catechism's* exposition of the function of the homily can certainly be used to support a return to the instructional sermon. There is one definition of the homily in the *Catechism:* "an exhortation to accept this Word as what it truly is, the Word of God, and put it into practice" (#1349). Curiously, in the *Catechism's* English language index, the word "homily" refers the reader not to this definition but a description of the "deposit" of Christian moral teaching that "has been handed on, a deposit of a characteristic body of rules, commandments, and virtues proceeding from faith in Christ and animated by charity."[36] This preference for the instructional nature of the homily is also found in part Two, The Celebration of the Christian Mystery, which states that the liturgy is "the privileged place for catechizing the People of God" (#1074). The *Catechism* does state that the homily "extends" the proclamation of the gospel (#1154) but it does not contain Vatican II's kerygmatic or mystagogic definition: "a proclamation of God's wonderful works in the history of salvation, which is the mystery of Christ ever made present and active in us, especially in the celebration of the liturgy" (*SC*, 35). The *Catechism* seems to rely not on Paul VI's evangelical emphasis but on John Paul II's catechetical understanding of the homily.

There are a number of pastoral responses to the question of how the image of the teacher can be preserved in our preaching tradition: *(1) provide preaching syllabi that parcel out church teaching over a three-year period, corresponding to the three-year liturgical cycle of Scripture readings; (2) give an instruction following the prayer after communion; (3) let teaching naturally emerge in the homily from the biblical and liturgical texts.*

1) *Preaching syllabi*

In some U.S. dioceses preaching guides are designed to parcel out the content of the new catechism by corresponding it to the lectionary readings. This is a daunting task since, as we shall see in the next chapter, the Lectionary was not designed around a systematic presentation of the theological teachings of the Church but the proclamation of the paschal mystery of Christ. Gerard Sloyan, pioneer in the liturgical movement in the United States, strongly warns of the dangers of what some have called "lectionary catechesis":

> Any proposal to divide up the Catechism as the subject of pulpit instruction during the eucharistic celebration is to be deplored utterly. Such a program understands neither liturgy nor catechesis. It would rob Catholics of their biblical heritage yet again and only doubtfully instruct them.[37]

The great danger of lectionary catechesis is that the preacher might ignore the scriptural readings or liturgical mystery in order to comply to a topical series. Prior to Vatican II we often had the ludicrous situation when, on the third Sunday of Advent, the text, "I am the voice . . . ." (John 1:25), became the springboard for the topic, God Speaks to Us Through Tradition, and the text, "I will, be thou made clean" (Matt 8:3), from the third Sunday after Epiphany, was taken for the subject, The Sixth and Ninth Commandments. Besides the danger of using the Scripture as a springboard for instruction, there is also the lamentable habit of some homilists who say "a few words" on the Scripture readings and then proceed to give a long instruction which is almost a verbatim rendering of the *Catechism*. Such "double sermons" are confusing and usually dull because they do not open up the Word in an imaginative and pastoral manner that is connected to the liturgical celebration. The liturgy should not be viewed as a convenient platform for doctrinal and moral instruction. To do so would be to violate Vatican II's claim that the homily is "part of the liturgy itself" (*SC*, 52). The council made this claim to counter some liturgical authors in the 1960s who were still referring to preaching as an "interruption at Mass" or "accidental to the Mass."

2) *Instruction after the Communion prayer*

Charles Miller proposes what he calls a "helpful compromise" which preserves instruction during the liturgy without violating Vatican II's definition of the homily. He proposes that the homily be kept "within a reasonable time limit" so that a series of instructions can be given following the prayer after Communion. Miller writes:

> It is an ideal time for teaching, but the presentation must be within a time limit of no more than five minutes. Much can be said in a well organized presentation, even if it is brief. The priest need not give this instruction himself; any qualified person may do so . . . . This compromise, although not perfect, meets the requirement of law regarding a homily and the need for instruction.[38]

Charles Miller is correct. His compromise is not perfect. It still leaves the impression that the liturgy is a convenient platform for a lecture. The primary purpose of the entire liturgical action is to lead the assembly to lift up their hearts, not fill up their minds. Parish missions, the church bulletin, Bible study groups, parish lecture series, and academic courses sponsored by parishes are natural places for formal catechesis. Our Catholic tradition never had a built-in space for formal catechesis similar to the adult Sunday school in many Protestant communities. But we could create new possibilities like a Pastor's Forum following a particular Mass for those in the congregation who wish and need to receive more formal training.

3) *Teaching that naturally emerges from the biblical and liturgical texts*

The first Christians did not preach one message and teach another. In the New Testament the *kērygma* was the content of both.

Preaching and teaching dealt with the action and the word of God, the call and promise of God in Christ. We have seen how in the early Church there was a systematic presentation of the mysteries of Christ given to the newly baptized in the post-baptismal preaching known as mystagogy. The liturgical celebration of the sacraments served as the primary source of theology. Samuel E. Torvend imagines:

> If one were to ask an Ephrem, a Chrysostom, or an Ambrose, "What does it mean to be a Christian?" one most likely would *not* be invited to an inquiry class or given a religious tract but taken in hand to the celebration of the Easter Vigil, in effect being told: if you want to know the meaning of the Christian life come and see how Christians are made.[39]

We must not confuse mystagogic catechesis, which is organic to the Church's worship, with formal catechesis. The purpose of the first is transformation and takes place in church. The purpose of the second is information and takes places in a classroom. When St. Paul spoke of "instruction" he used the term not as "classroom instruction," but rather "spiritual instruction" or wisdom. Daniel Patte reminds us:

> Paul's proclamation of the gospel therefore involves both repetition of the *kērygma in its Jewish vocabulary,* and a declaration to his hearers and readers of its fulfillment *in terms of their own experience* . . . [i]n the proclamation of Paul's gospel a preacher does not have the responsibility of proving the truth of the message—God does it. The preacher's primary responsibility is to witness to God's fulfillment of the gospel.[40]

FIYH clearly states that the homily does not "primarily concern itself with a systematic theological understanding of the faith. The liturgical gathering is not primarily an educational assembly" (17–8).

Gerard Sloyan has offered the strongest rationale for letting teaching naturally emerge in the liturgy. He points out:

> Liturgy is chiefly worship, the prayer of the community. While it instructs it does so only incidentally. It is intended to worship, to give thanks, to ask, to plead, to importune. The lectionary readings and the homily are not an instructive interlude in worship. They *are* worship, worshipful words.[41]

The entire liturgy naturally instructs not just in Bible proclamation and preaching but in every gesture, every prayer, every symbol of celebration.

Arguing from tradition, Sloyan believes "that the best assurance that the ancient faith will be preserved and promoted in the hearing of believers is that the Bible be preached at the Sunday liturgy in and out of season."[42] He is sensitive to the pastor who is concerned that church teaching might be ignored. Ignorance of what we do and do not believe about the incarnation, how the Triune Godhead indwells the baptized, why the sacraments are channels of grace are vitally important for the Christian. But Sloyan believes that the perceptive preacher who consistently thinks biblically will have no problem in making relationships with existential realities and the Church's theological traditions. He proposes:

> The preacher who genuinely fears, after having preached the three-year cycle four or five times, that certain doctrinal or ethical developments of the centuries are getting short shrift . . . should sit down and carefully plot a correction of the omissions over the next few months. This cannot be done, of course, without serious study of the upcoming texts.[43]

We have reviewed the image of the herald and the teacher in the Catholic preaching tradition. In the New Testament we treasure the images of Jesus as herald and teacher. But Willard Jabusch reminds us: "The Gospel was 'proclaimed' not so much through oratory, even Semitic oratory, as through discussion, questions, answers, homely examples and friendly conversation." As for Jesus the teacher, Jabusch observes:

> The mystery of the kingdom of God was not presented in an ordered and logical way . . . with the deductions of the philosopher or the relentless drive of the lawyer, the precision of the engineer or the clarity of the mathematician. The clarity of the gospel was the clarity of the poet; the words of Christ were the warm and colorful words of the artist.[44]

It is to the image of the perceptive preacher who is poet and artist that we now turn: the interpreter.

The Interpreter

Borrowing the classic triad of Cicero, St. Augustine wrote that the purpose of preaching was (1) to teach *(docere);* (2) to delight *(delectare);* (3) to persuade *(flectere)*.[45] When we teach, we offer information. When we delight, we elicit a satisfying emotional response from our listeners. When we delight, we inspire and touch the hearts of people. When we preachers persuade, we move people to action about their behavior. While the homily is meant to teach, it is also meant to delight and move. The Tridentine preaching reforms unfortunately reduced the purpose of preaching to two elements, teaching and persuading.[46] The image of the preacher as interpreter was not prominent because the emphasis on delight was muted.

Aristotle recognized three types of oratory: (1) *political* which took place in the senate and sought to convince the assembly to take a certain course of action through persuasion and dissuasion; (2) *forensic* which took place in the courtroom and involved accusation and defense of a criminal; (3) *epideictic* which was heard during ceremonial occasions by speakers who attempted to arouse the sentiments of wonder, gratitude, love, and the desire for imitation. Political speech looked to the future while forensic speech was geared to the past. The time-frame for epideictic speech was the present.[47] Epideictic speakers sought to describe (interpret) their world through praise and blame. John O'Malley's research demonstrates how the papal court preachers in Renaissance Rome effectively used epideictic rhetoric in their sermons during Mass.[48] There are traces of concern for epideictic preaching in Trent's use of such phrases as "impressing upon them with briefness and plainness of speech the vice that they must avoid and the virtues they must cultivate" (Fifth Session, c. 2). But concern for orthodoxy and refutation of heresies plus moral exhortation eventually stifled this emphasis.

In chapter 1 we pointed to the image of the preacher found in *FIYH,* the interpreter. The preacher is described not primarily as a teacher but a "mediator of meaning" who attends to the biblical text and the pastoral context in order to offer the liturgical assembly "a scriptural interpretation of human existence" which enables the community "to recognize God's active presence in faith through liturgical word and gesture, and beyond the liturgical assembly, through life lived in conformity with the Gospel" (7 and 29).

FIYH's emphasis on the preacher as one who mediates meaning in a way in which listeners "can recognize their own concerns and God's concern for them" restores the ancient tradition of epideictic speech and the aim of "to delight" from St. Augustine's classic preaching triad.[49] Lawrence Rosenfield speaks of the need for words upon encountering mystery. He believes that with epideictic oratory, the ancients sought to illumine the presence of Being radiating within virtuous citizens for the ennoblement of life and the good of the polis.[50] Drawing upon Rosenfield's analysis, James Schmitmeyer sees the dual focus on the divine and human found in epideictic genre to be in harmony with *FIYH*'s definition of preaching as a speaking event which strives to speak the truth of God's presence in relation to a community's lived experience.[51]

Emphasis on the preacher as interpreter, who employs present tense language, also emerges from contemporary homiletic thought. David Buttrick begins his *Homiletic* by focusing on the descriptive quality of preaching or "naming a world."[52] In constructing a theology of proclamation, Mary Catherine Hilkert speaks of preaching as "naming grace."[53]

The introduction of the interpretive element of the homily by *FIYH* retrieves an important aspect of synagogue preaching missing in conciliar and post-conciliar documents on the nature of the homily. Yngve Brilioth noted three basic elements in Jesus' sermon in the synagogue at Nazareth (Luke 4:15-30). First it was *liturgical* since it was part of the Jewish service. Second, it was *exegetical* because it was spoken from a biblical text. Third, it was *prophetic* since it spoke to the present by transforming the historical revelation into a contemporaneous, dynamic reality: "Today this scripture passage is fulfilled in your hearing." When Brilioth referred to the prophetic element of Jesus' sermon, he was speaking of an act of interpretation.[54]

What shaped the prophetic nature of Jesus' preaching was the tradition of Judaism which hoped for the reign of God at the last day when God would come to judge the living and the dead and set up a kingdom of justice and peace. But Jesus announced to the people that they did not have to wait for the last day of *shalom* to arrive since God was already breaking into their lives: "The time is fulfilled and the kingdom of God has come near; repent, and believe in the good news" (Mark 1:15). Jesus interpreted the events and lives of the people in light of God's immanent reign. He preached in a way that gave insight into his followers' lives. He began with the common occurrences of people and invited them to dig deeply into the ordinary to experience the finger of God. He invited people to interpret the signs of the times, even when those signs were as tiny as mustard seeds. As Jesus interpreted, values were turned upside down, deadbeats came to the center of the kingdom while the powerful were warned about their complacency and failure to read the signs of the times.

FIYH lists three contemporary sources for the image of the inter-preter as "mediator of meaning": *(1) communication studies; (2) the eccle-siology advanced by Vatican II's Dogmatic Constitution of the Church; (3) the sacramental, relational approach to revelation found in the Dogmatic Constitution on Divine Revelation.* Two more sources should also be considered: *(4) a new appreciation of preaching as a ministry of meaning; (5) a sensitivity to imaginative language.*

1) *Communication studies*

The document contends that the oral presentation of a single per-son is not a particularly effective way of bringing about a change in attitude or behavior. It is, however, effective in making explicit or re-inforcing attitudes previously held. The homily, therefore, "will be less effective as a means of instruction and/or exhortation than of inter-pretation—that is, as a means of enabling people to recognize the im-plications, in liturgy and in life, of the faith that is already theirs" (26).

2) *Ecclesiology*

The document pays serious attention to the liturgical assembly where the primary reality is not the necessary offices and ministries but Christ in the assembly, the People of God. Preaching is not only a matter of interpreting the Scripture but interpreting the lives of the liturgical gathering. Here the document stresses the "oneness to the Lord's voice not only in the Scriptures but in the events of our daily lives and in the experience of our brothers and sisters" (10). While the teacher tells the people what they do not know about God, the interpreter tells them that God is already in their lives. The inter-preter gives names and images to the grace and demons of our lives. Thus, the tone of the liturgy changes from an event where the preacher educates the uncertified to what Aidan Kavanagh has called "the hearing of the gospel out loud, so to speak, among one's peers in faith."[55]

3) *Revelation*

FIYH abandons the propositional notion of revelation that had dominated Roman Catholic theology since Vatican I. Revelation had been understood as a body of truths beyond the grasp of reason that had to be accepted because of the authority of the one revealing them.

The bishops' document presents a relational theology of revelation found in *DV*: the one mystery of the Word of God has been entrusted to the "entire holy people, united to its pastors" (10). *FIYH* states that "the preacher does not so much attempt to explain the Scriptures as to interpret the human situation through the Scriptures" (20). James Wallace has written that in *FIYH* "[t]he purpose of the text, biblical or liturgical, the value of the tradition, of past or present official formulations, is to help identify how God is acting *now* in the life of this community. The Scripture is there as a medium for identifying the presence of God here and now."[56]

One of the distinguishing marks of contemporary Catholic theology is, in David Tracy's words, a quest for a mutual correlation between "Christian texts and common human experience and language."[57] It is a quest that leads theologians to see what is in front of their noses as they ponder the Christian Story. Mary Catherine Hilkert explores a theology of proclamation from a Catholic perspective of grace as active in and through humanity and describes revelation in sacramental terms. She draws upon Karl Rahner's "world of grace" and Edward Schillebeeckx's "contrast experience" to show how revelation is located within human experience. Rahner found the locus of revelation in the transcendental depths of the human person. For Schillebeeckx, that locus is found in history. Hilkert builds her theology of proclamation upon the work of both these theologians whose profound concern for the credibility of the Christian faith and the proclamation of the gospel in the contemporary world calls us to preaching as an act of interpretation:

> The role of the preacher is to bring the depth dimension of the mystery of human existence as God's self-offer of love to explicit expression through interpreting that experience in the light of the scriptures, the liturgy, and the whole of the Christian tradition. Thus preaching draws the hearers of the word into a deeper relationship with God that is at the same time a deeper experience of their everyday human life and relationships as graced.[58]

The image of the preacher as interpreter found in *FIYH* resonates with Karl Rahner's understanding of "the liturgy of the world" which we explored in chapter 1. Rahner reportedly had problems with Vatican II's claim that the Church's liturgy is the source or summit of our lives. "Rahner presumed that while the summit of our self-surrender could take place in the liturgy, it normally takes place in the midst of ordinary, daily life and is then manifested and expressed in the liturgy."[59] In Rahner's "liturgy of the world" the preacher's task is to reveal a hidden God, to trace the footsteps of the Trinity in the midst of ordinary, daily life. Michael Skelley sums up Rahner's liturgical thought: "If we cannot see God in the ordinary events of our daily life, both the bad and the good, we cannot expect that we will suddenly be able to see God when we gather for worship."[60] Rahner saw the task of the preacher not so much as offering information about God but revealing the God already present in people's lives. Criticizing sermons that dogmatized and moralized, he believed that the reason many people leave the Church is "because the language flowing from the pulpit has no meaning for them; it has no connection with their own life and simply bypasses many threatening and unavoidable issues."[61]

4) *Ministry of Meaning*

FIYH's use of the term "mediator of meaning" to describe the interpretive element of preaching resonates with our contemporary search for a definition of ministry. There are many tasks in ministry. But ministers now recognize that others in the religious and the secular community also perform these tasks as well. Many are teachers, heralds, witnesses to the faith. David Buttrick puts it bluntly:

> The *primary* task of ministry is not caring, for all kinds of people can offer devoted care; nor is it counseling, for there are able professionals who counsel; nor is it church management, for managers abound. No, the primary task of ministry is *meaning*.[62]

5) *A New Language*

Fred Craddock's "New Homiletic" was influenced by his recognition of the effect of television which has "changed [the] shape the human sensorium" from oral to visual. "In the opinion of some," he writes, "the success of the Christian proclamation depends upon the church's ability to make the transition so men [sic] can *see*."[63]

The language of the teacher is chosen to instruct. It can be dry, highly abstract, and not designed to delight and to move the heart. The language of the herald can be sloganistic and repetitive. The herald does not have to search for the most effective words and images, just repeat the message from on high. Gerard Sloyan dubs the language of some preachers "Religionspeak." It is the "tongue of a land with no known inhabitants."[64] But the interpreter's task is to struggle to find just the right word and image that will capture that message. The interpreter is like the poet, which was Rahner's favorite metaphor for the priest. He often chastised theologians and preachers of his day for becoming prosaic. He believed that "where the word of God says what is most sublime and plunges this most deeply into man's [sic] hearts, there is also to be found a pregnant word of human poetry."[65]

FIYH's description of the preacher as one who interprets "the signs of the times" by offering specific language and images for the grace and demons of our lives responds to Rahner's search for "a pregnant word of human poetry." The document insists:

> Whatever its form, the function of the Eucharistic homily is to enable people to lift up their hearts, to praise and thank the Lord for his presence in their lives. It will do this more effectively if the language it uses is specific, graphic, and imaginative. The more we can turn to the picture language of the poet and the storyteller, the more we will be able to preach in a way that invites people to respond from the heart as well as from the mind (25).

The preacher's "pregnant word of human poetry" is not complicated or embellished speech nor second-rate verse. David Buttrick reminds us that the vocabulary of the New Testament's *koinē* Greek is not much more than five thousand words. He also reminds us that in the troubling and profound moments in our lives, we often revert to simple words. Buttrick advises:

> If our constructions are commonplace and our phrases clichéd, we will speak a language suited for the well-lit center of life and, thereby, translate the gospel into conventional wisdom; we will be trite. But simple words can be put together in astonishing ways. Words can combine the magic of metaphor. Words can sing a simple beauty. Words can be packed with concrete stuff of life so that, with vividness, we can see what is spoken . . . . With simple words we can wander into Presence.[66]

Although the image of the preacher as interpreter is relatively new to Catholic homilists, there are three convincing reasons to highlight this image, especially in our times: It *(1) pays serious attention to the specific context of preaching; (2) encourages a prayerful and imaginative preparation of the homily; (3) preserves the prophetic nature of the homily.*

1) *Pays serious attention to the specific context of preaching*

During the Roman Synod of Bishops on evangelization, there was a serious debate about the role of preaching in the post-Vatican II Church. Some bishops urged a return to the catechetical sermons popular before the council which offered a systematic presentation of church teaching. There were other bishops at the synod, however, who questioned a return to the catechetical sermon. One bishop summed up their position well when he said, "What is needed now in our world and church is not an explanation of God but an experience of God." We sometimes think that just because we have offered information to people, we have solved a problem. But, as Søren Kierkegaard noted, "there is no lack of information in the Christian land, something else is lacking."[67]

The bishops of the Second Vatican Council suspected that the "something else lacking" in the preaching of the Church was the failure to preach the gospel in the context of the "concrete circumstances of life." The bishops insisted that "preaching must not present God's Word in a general and abstract fashion" (*PO,* 4). A homily might be exegetically and theologically sound and precise but if it fails to reveal and name grace in the specific context of listeners' lives, then the Good News is not heard. The preacher as interpreter values the assembly's particular issues, events, seasons, characters, questions, addictions, struggles, and blessings. The preacher as interpreter attends to the *sensus* and *tempus fidelium.* That is what the writers of the gospels did: they told the story of Christ's paschal mystery in the specific context of the story of their listeners.

Walter Burghardt, who describes himself as a "weaver of words," challenges the didactic and abstract Catholic preaching style inherited from the instructional sermons of the past with a vocabulary dominated by abstract nouns ending in *ion.* Notice how he preaches in the "concrete circumstances of life":

> Moreover, there is so much evil and injustice over the globe that we grow used to it. We were shocked when TV first brought war into our living rooms; now we can wolf our pizzas and slurp our Schlitz to the roar of rockets and the flow of blood. It's commonplace; we see too much of it; it's part of the human tragedy. It no longer grabs our guts—no more than broken bodies in the Orange Bowl.[68]

It is the task of the interpreter, the poet, the artist, the prophet to be specific, to pay attention to the details because God hides in the details. *FIYH* encourages homilists to be specific in their interpretation of human existence in light of the Scriptures: "The preacher represents this community by voicing its concerns, by naming its demons, and thus enabling it to gain some understanding and control of the evil which afflicts it" (7).

2) *Encourages a prayerful and imaginative preparation of the homily*

The image of the preacher as interpreter challenges the highly rationalistic, scientific approach found in much of contemporary biblical and theological scholarship. We often approach the liturgical texts not as poets but as technocrats. But technology is incapable of revealing Being. That is the vocation of the artist and poet. The technician seeks to capture reality while the artist and poet try to reveal it. The preacher must not only know how many Isaiahs there were but also capture the prophetic vision and savor the powerful images of the Isaiahs.

FIYH encourages a prayerful reading of the Scriptures in the preparation of the homily. While the document encourages homilists to study scholarly methods of biblical interpretation, it discourages running to the "experts" (commentaries, homily services) too early in the process. "By doing so we block out the possibility of letting these texts speak to us and to the concerns we share with a congregation" (32). The images and words of Scripture are prayed over early in the week so that they might be noticed throughout the week in the specific circumstances of life. Like the poet and artist, nothing should escape the preacher's attention. Elizabeth Barrett Browning reminded us that

> Earth's crammed with heaven,
> And every common bush afire with God:
> But only he who sees, takes off his shoes. . . .[69]

The image of the preacher as interpreter introduced to us in *FIYH* has deep roots in the Catholic homiletic tradition. St. Thomas Aquinas, known for his systematic treatment of theology, was also a poet who wrote hymns. He once told a friend, "I have seen things that make all my writings seem like straw."[70] He defined the preacher as one "who shares the fruit of his contemplation with others."[71] The preacher as interpreter shares with the assembly not just information about God but *who* and *where* God is in our lives. The preacher gives to the people the gifts of insight, poetic language, and contemplation.

3) *Preserves the prophetic nature of the homily*

Our liturgy by its very nature demands that we take seriously both a God who liberates and reconciles as well as a world which groans because it has yet to be liberated and reconciled. Our worship is oriented to the sanctification of individual worshippers and to *koinonia* with all creation. Since the homily is an interpretation of life, the homilist must necessarily be an interpreter of the particular culture in which we live.

Culture is a revelation system. "It quietly converts, elicits commitments, transforms, provides heroics, suggests human fulfillments. The culture, then, is a gospel—a book of revelation—mediating beliefs, revealing us to ourselves."[72] Robert Bellah and his colleagues tell us that culture creates in us what Alexis de Tocqueville once called "habits of the heart."[73] Bellah and other sociologists observe that ours is a secular world that is pluralistic and relativistic. Four particular characteristics mark our culture in the United States: affluence, individualism, a therapeutic approach to problem-solving, and an ambiguity about our power.[74] Recent sociological studies of the religious habits of Roman Catholics reveal highly privatized notions of worship and Church.[75] The social encyclicals, the pastoral letters of the U.S. Bishops on the economy and peace, the preaching of recent popes about the poor and disenfranchised have yet to make a major impact on the way we preach and worship. David Buttrick believes that "we must be willing to take on cultural assumptions that are no longer viable: our blind faith in technological progress, our reliance on the power of death . . . the all-pervasive 'triumph of the therapeutic,' and other cultural idols."[76]

The preacher has three options for touching the habits of the heart of a particular liturgical assembly. In the first, the preacher can simply ignore those habits and preach homilies "for all times" which say nothing to anyone in any time. We have observed how one of the shortcomings of the image of the preacher as herald is the timeless nature of the herald's message that ignores the particular context of the congregation. One of the major reasons why some preachers do not deal with a particular culture's habits of the heart is because they do not believe that they are the locus of God's revelation. For example, Karl Barth believed that preaching must aim "beyond the hill of relevance"[77] because we "must preach the Bible and nothing else."[78] He lived to regret that while he was a parish preacher during

World War I he never mentioned the war in his sermons.[79] In the dialectical imagination of Barth, revelation is totally God's action. Therefore, preachers need not attempt an interpretation of a culture's habits of the heart but simply reiterate the biblical text. The first option emphasizes a dialectical rather than a Catholic sacramental or incarnational theology of revelation.

The second homiletic option is to engage a culture's habits of the heart but with the bias of theological dualism. The world is not to be trusted since it is the devil's playground. Preaching here becomes a matter of denouncing habits of the heart rather than seeing them as possible encounters with God's self-expression or grace. In his first speech at the opening of the Second Vatican Council, Pope John XXIII denounced the "prophets of gloom" who were unwilling to renew the Church by reading the "signs of the times." The last document of the council, the Pastoral Constitution on the Church in the Modern World, reflects the "grief and anguish" of the people of our time but also proclaims *gaudium et spes* (joy and hope). Thus, our Catholic tradition which says the homily leads us to "lift up our hearts" would find unacceptable this second homiletic option.

The third and only acceptable option the homilist has is to engage a particular culture's habits of the heart with both the balm and challenge of the gospel. Preaching becomes not a matter of ignoring or denouncing the world but confronting it with the gospel's power to transform. Walter Brueggemann has proposed that contemporary preaching should be "a poetic construal of an alternative world."[80] He uses the term "poetic" to describe the prophetic speech of the Bible.

Walter Burghardt has cautioned against two extremes in the task of prophetic preaching: "manipulation of the Mass in the interests of ideologies" and "a perilous conservatism that would make the liturgy utterly inoffensive, a peaceful Sunday service where oppressed and oppressor can escape from the furies and passions of the week, simply praise God for His wonderful works."[81] The image of the preacher as interpreter helps avoid the two extremes of which Burghardt warns.

The interpreter does not manipulate in the interest of ideologies but offers a fresh vision of what life might look like. Church social teaching can easily become nagging moralism in the pulpit. We sometimes think that the only way to preach the just word is by a confrontational or critical stance. But Paul Scott Wilson believes: "The prophetic ministry is also the dreaming ministry. Prophets provide dreams of what human society could conceivably be, redemptive dreams that point us in new directions away from the nightmares of the past."[82] What moves us to justice is not a didactic lesson but a new vision, a new picture, a fresh juxtaposition which gives us a new way of seeing in the dark. Prophets are poets who use words and images to help create a new vision of justice and peace. Walter Brueggemann believes that:

> The new conversation, on which our very lives depend, requires a poet and not a moralist. Because finally church people are like other people; we are not changed by new rules. The deep places in our lives—places of resistance and embrace—are not ultimately reached by instruction. Those places of resistance and embrace are reached only by stories, by images, metaphors, and phrases that line out the world differently, apart from our fear and hurt. The reflection that comes from the poet requires playfulness, imagination, and interpretation.[83]

Because interpreters pay attention to the details and context of preaching, they cannot escape from the "furies and passions of the week." Pope John Paul II, in his homily at a Mass in Santo Domingo in 1979, spoke of a world in which "no more children lack sufficient nutrition, education, instruction . . . no more poor peasants without land . . . no more workers mistreated . . . no more systems which permit the exploitation of man by man [sic] or by the state."[84] Interpreters are compelled to utter the just word and to do so not in vague and general terms but in specifics.

Before leaving this reflection on the image of the preacher as interpreter, we should also consider three caveats: *(1) interpretation is a communal affair; (2) interpretation may be clouded by faulty diagnosis; (3) interpretation is a risky business.*

1) *Interpretation is a communal affair*

While it is true that the preacher, like the poet and artist, needs a sacred cave for the quiet and space required of art, the homily is a proclamation that arises out of and celebrates the gifts of God in the assembly. A preacher isolated from the concerns and needs of the assembly and the Church's theological tradition fails in the act of interpretation. *FIYH* presents the ideal of a homilist preparing a homily by listening to the community:

> In order to make such connections between the lives of the people and the Gospel, the preacher will have to be a listener before he is

a speaker. Listening is not an isolated moment. It is a way of life. It means openness to the Lord's voice not only in the Scriptures but in the events of our daily lives and in the experience of our brothers and sisters. It is not just *my* listening but *our* listening together for the Lord's word to the community (10).

It is not an easy task to read the signs of the times. There are conflicting voices. A preacher can get locked into either a bleak or overly optimistic picture of our times. The opening line of *Gaudium et spes* balances both "the joy and hope" with the "grief and anguish" of the people of our age. A preacher who is isolated from the community, the tradition, teaching and prayer of the Church, literature, popular culture, media, political struggles, the violence and new possibilities of our times, will not feed people with fresh bread.

2) *Interpretation may be clouded by faulty diagnosis*

When Peter arrived at the house of Cornelius, the centurion, his host fell to his feet and began to worship Peter. Peter would have none of this. "But Peter made him get up, saying, 'Stand up; I am only a mortal'" (Acts 10:26). There have been many times in the history of the Church when preachers forgot their own mortality. We preachers make mistakes, sometimes about the most elementary notions of life. Interpretation always begins with diagnosis, i.e., an understanding about the way things are. But often there are forces in our culture, our personalities, our theological dispositions that cloud a healthy biblical diagnosis.

Jean Delumeau catalogued many of the sermons of hellfire and damnation during the medieval era which led to an unhealthy preoccupation with death and the macabre and dangerous psychological problems such as extreme guilt and scrupulosity. Delumeau traces the origin of these sermons to the excessive use of the doctrine of "contempt for the world."[85] Fr. Charles Coughlin (1891–1979) was second only to President Roosevelt as a radio orator in the 1930s. In the early days of the Depression, his radio sermons conveyed compassion and communicated hope. But his personal anti-Semitic bias clouded his interpretation of life.

What influences in our own day cloud our homiletic interpretation? For example, are we aware that like the people for whom we preach, we too are influenced by the modern-scientific-industrial view of life that puts great stock in the capacity to know, control, and manage?

Walter Brueggemann believes that this model "which lies at the heart of the American perception of reality and which shapes most of our institutions, clearly resists the good news of the gospel, for it is based on the assumption that graciousness must be banished."[86]

3) *Interpretation is a risky business*

In the play *Mass Appeal*, Fr. Tim Farley cautions the young deacon Mark Dolson about beginning his homily with: "Jesus is not impressed with your mink hats and your cashmere coats and your blue hair. . . ." Father Farley warns Mark, "If it's not their position, they'll turn on you." Mark shoots back, "Then the only reason you give sermons is to be liked?" The pastor replies, "I like being liked. It gives me a warm feeling." At the end of the play, the teacher is transformed into the student. Father Farley learns something about himself as minister and preacher. In his final homily he tells the people: "From here—I haven't really been a very good priest to you. From here—I never really cared enough to run the risk of loosing you."[87]

Jesus' homily in the synagogue of Nazareth was an interpretation of life that aroused his neighbor's wrath because he dared to say that God's visitation and salvation were not just for them but for the poor and oppressed of all nations. That is why they tried to drive him out of town and throw him over a cliff (Luke 4:29). There is never a guarantee that our interpretation of life will gain us peace, security, and a happy relationship with the community. Because both preacher and congregation are at varying degrees of personal growth, theological sophistication, and faith, there is always the danger that the preacher's interpretation will be misunderstood or rejected. The ecclesial nature of the liturgy as praise to God, its focus on the paschal mystery of Christ, and the invocation of the Holy Spirit will not guarantee that our homiletic interpretations will be risk free but will help protect us from homilies that are merely "of human origin" (Gal 1:11).

The Witness

Our fourth image for the preacher does not come from the normative liturgical documents concerning preaching. It is found, however, in Pope Paul VI's exhortation On Evangelization in the Modern World in which he describes our present time as one that "thirsts for authenticity." He is particularly sensitive to young people who "have a horror of the artificial or false" and "are searching above all for truth and honesty."[88] Paul VI seeks to complement the image of the teacher, long entrenched in the Catholic tradition, with the image of the witness:

> Modern man [sic] listens more willingly to witnesses than to teachers, and if he does listen to teachers, it is because they are witnesses . . . the world is calling for evangelizers to speak to it of a God whom the evangelists themselves should know and be familiar with as if they could see the invisible.[89]

FIYH refers to a survey taken among a group of parishioners in which they were asked what they hoped to experience during a homily. "When the results were in, the answer was clear. What the majority wanted was simply to hear a person of faith speaking" (15).

Despite this finding and Paul VI's clear call for us to be witnesses to the gospel in our times, most Catholics seem uncomfortable about the role. Witness conjures up images of the overly eager evangelist preaching on the street corner or the born-again Christian gushing slogans on a religious television program. The Catholic homiletic texts of yesterday warned about using personal pronouns in our sermons. We were not to allow our own story to eclipse the story of God. We were urged to preach Christ, not ourselves.

Contemporary homileticians and theologians are divided in their opinion about giving personal witness or testimony in preaching. The title of Richard Thulin's book *The "I" of the Sermon* suggests that a storm is raging around the issue of first-person singular narrative as a vehicle for the proclamation of God's word.[90] One school sees no reason for the preacher's personal references from the pulpit. David Buttrick believes that personal references in preaching "split consciousness." He writes, "To be blunt, there are virtually no good reasons to talk about ourselves from the pulpit."[91] While systematic theologian Catherine Mowry LaCugna spoke of the need for the homilist to employ concrete "examples and applications of the Gospel," she proposed an unyielding rubric: "Personal references should be avoided because they set up the preacher as the norm for the community's experience of faith." She found such references "highly distracting and ineffective."[92]

Such homiletic advice about the dangers of personal witness in preaching seems to reflect a dialectical theology of revelation which emphasizes the paradoxical distance between God and the world rather than toward a Catholic sacramental or incarnational theology of revelation which emphasizes God's immanence. In the sacramental imagination God's presence is found hidden within all of human life (including the preacher's) as illuminated by the Scriptures. Mary Catherine Hilkert captures the sacramental perspective: "[I]f preachers are to announce the gospel of Jesus Christ and not 'some other gospel,' they must listen to human experience with an ear for 'an echo of the gospel.'"[93]

Most contemporary homileticians take a middle-ground position concerning the use of personal references in the homily. They recognize the dangers of such preaching deteriorating into narcissism and self-aggrandizement. The pulpit can become a convenient niche for navel-gazing, working out clerical problems of authority or loneliness, or for masking our anger and prejudices, and for parading our wit and theological talents.

But a homilist's experiences, both mighty and mundane, are part of the stuff of life that needs to be interpreted in light of the Scriptures. If employed well, they need not be distracting nor eclipse the gospel. Indeed, they could be most effective in helping a community to recognize its own experience of the Good News. Walter J. Burghardt makes a helpful distinction here when he writes about the "delicate line between the 'I' that stirs others to think and tell their own story, and the 'I' that embarrasses, that makes others mumble uncomfortably, 'I'm sorry for your troubles, Father.'"[94]

The image of the preacher as witness can be argued from (1) *tradition;* (2) *authority;* (3) *effective communication.*

1) *Tradition*

The image of the witness is deeply rooted in the biblical tradition. God is invoked as a witness against the crimes of Israel (Jer 29:23; Mic 3:8; Mal 3:5). At the conclusion of Luke's Gospel, Jesus commands his disciples to proclaim the gospel to all nations because they are witnesses of his suffering, death, and resurrection (Luke 24:46-48). The call to conversion in the New Testament is closely tied to witness. Ronald Witherup has written that in the Gospel of John conversion "comes from a personal encounter with Jesus but can begin with the testimony of others who believe."[95]

None of us have seen God the way the disciples saw God in Jesus, but we are still called to be witnesses of the paschal mystery.

We sometimes think that the only thing we are called to share in our preaching is what we know. But the biblical image of witness reminds us that we are also called to share what we have seen. God did not ask the prophet Amos what he knew but what he saw (Amos 7:8).

Faith has always depended upon analogy. Personal analogues need not be self-serving. They have the possibility of igniting faith. Preachers have always struggled to find in their own life glimpses of God that can be shared with others so that what is particular can become universal. An example of this can be found in two sentences by William Sloane Coffin:

> As a boy, I loved to go puddle gazing, wandering from one puddle to the next, wondering how so much of the sky could be reflected in such small bodies of water. Today I often marvel at how so much of the story of heaven and earth is captured in small biblical tales such as the story of Jesus and the paralytic.[96]

If we took the rubric about avoiding personal references seriously, we would have to expunge Dr. King's "I Have a Dream" speech (which is an adaptation of a sermon) of all references to "*I* Have a Dream." We would have to excise whole chunks of the Bible. St. Paul would have to be cautioned against the dangers of his personal stories of ship-wrecks and thorns in his flesh. The prophets would be told that their personal references were distracting even though that is what prophets are supposed to do—distract. Jeremiah would be muzzled although he probably would still protest,

> "My anguish, my anguish! I writhe in pain!
>   Oh, the walls of my heart!
> My heart is beating wildly;
>   I cannot keep quiet" (Jer 4:19).

2) *Authority*

Richard L. Thulin has argued that appropriate use of personal story can give preachers authority in the pulpit because listeners are more open to preachers who attempt honestly to connect with the Good News. Thulin's reasoning is similar to the existential interpretation that Pope Paul VI gave when he said that people today listen more willingly to witnesses than to teachers. Thulin writes:

> People will not listen seriously to what a minister says simply because he or she is ordained and speaks with the authority of the church. Nor will people be receptive to what a minister says simply because she or he quotes from the Bible or from the writings of some significant theologian. What catches the ear and urges response is the voice of a living witness . . . . It is a voice of conviction supported by life story.[97]

This does not mean that every homily should contain a personal story, but that ideally every homily should arise from the personal convictions and witness of the homilist. The preacher must make use of many resources in homiletic preparation: prayer, Scripture, commentaries, literature, social analysis, the media, etc., but ultimately what gives the preacher authority in the pulpit is the personal conviction and witness that springs from contemplation.

3) *Effective communication*

Despite David Buttrick's claim that research shows that personal illustrations always split consciousness, he offers no empirical studies to prove his hypothesis. Other contemporary homileticians have argued the exact opposite position. Some have advocated the use of personal witness, especially when dealing with highly charged social, political, and ethical issues. Richard Jensen, for example, makes the point that personal witness has the potential of effective communication since it creates a distance which enables participation of the listeners:

> They can laugh at you, cry with you, disagree with you, etc. They have the space to do that . . . They can take you or leave you! They may finally identify strongly with your story and see in your story that is a decision freely made. You haven't forced it upon them.[98]

Three caveats concerning the image of the preacher as witness are in order: *(1) avoid the personal witness that embarrasses the congregation; (2) avoid the personal story that puts you in a favorable light; (3) avoid personal stories which do not intersect with the listeners' story and the story of God.*

1) *Avoid the personal witness that embarrasses the congregation*

We must not get the impression that when we give witness in the pulpit we have to bare the deepest secrets of our soul, confess our sins

and addictions as we would to a confessor, spiritual director, or thera-
pist. Remember Burghardt's caution about the "I" that embarrasses.
Richard Thulin has listed a variety of forms for personal witness that
the homilist might consider: illustration, reminiscence, confession,
and self-portrayal. Most of the personal witness that occurs in the
pulpit is illustration or reminiscence. They need not embarrass but
rather connect with the listener's own story. The quote from William
Sloane Coffin listed above is a simple reminiscence of childhood that
is not dissimilar to many his congregation might have had.

A preacher might use some simple event that was noticed during the
week that is illustrative of something deeper. Once, on the First Sunday
of Advent (B), I placed in a homily something I saw during the week
that intersected with the biblical readings and the liturgical season:

> On the way to school the other day,
>> I saw something that sparked my Advent hope.
> As I drove past an elementary school,
>> I saw a teacher with her small band of kids.
> The teacher wasn't helping them to put up Christmas lights
>> or a Santa Claus display.
> She was teaching them how to dig into the frozen ground
>> and plant tiny bulbs for the coming of spring . . . .
> She was teaching them something about expecting promises
>> to be fulfilled.
> The teacher is like the church
>> helping us to dig deeper into the meaning of our faith;
>> nudging us to take time during this anxious season
>> to plant some seeds of hope in our God
>> who is coming to save all people.[99]

2) *Avoid the personal story that puts you in a favorable light*

Dr. LaCugna's warning about the preacher becoming the norm of
the community's experience of faith should be heeded. Personal witness in the pulpit must not lead listeners to exclaim, "My God, the
preacher is perfect, I am not like that!" *FIYH* warns about preachers
"who speak ten feet above contradiction" (15).

John Killenger is wary of personal stories that place the preacher
in a favorable light. He writes, "Any story that represents the preacher
in an awkward or failing or fully human light is potentially helpful to
the cause of the sermon."[100] In other words, the personal story that

manifests faith in the midst of our own human struggles and foibles can be a powerful instrument of identification with our fellow pilgrims in the faith. It can also be an effective means of identifying with the stories of Scripture where most of the characters celebrated in God's story are like us.

3) *Avoid personal stories which do not intersect with the listeners' story and the story of God*

Elie Wiesel insists that each storyteller's tale is "fitted into the memory that is the living tradition of the people."[101] The aim of the preacher's personal story is not to disclose the heart of the preacher but the hearts of the listeners and the heart of God. The truth is always larger than the preacher's own experience of it because the preacher has inherited a rich treasure from the biblical and ecclesial traditions. An ideal homily is a weaving of three stories: the stories of the preacher, of God, and of the listener. The three-story model can serve as a grid to help evaluate our preaching.[102] This does not mean that each homily should contain $33^1/3$ percent of each story. There will be times when the story of the preacher will be explicit and times when it will be implicit. The question is not whether the homilist should use personal references, but how to do so in an appropriate manner that intersects with the listeners' story and the story of God.

Some Conclusions

We have seen how four major images of the homilist are rooted in the Catholic preaching tradition: *the herald, the teacher, the interpreter, the witness.* Only on rare occasions does a text or document on preaching mention all four. An exception is the 1994 *Directory on the Ministry and Life of Priests,* which speaks of priests as having the duty to interpret the "signs of the times" in the light of faith.[103] The *Directory* also states that priests are "not only witnesses, but also heralds and transmitters of the faith (teachers)."[104]

Ultimately it is the preacher with the pastoral heart in dialogue with a particular assembly who must decide which image is appropriate for particular liturgical celebrations, seasons, biblical texts, local and national contexts, and pastoral needs. There are times when what is needed is the herald's voice, especially when in sad times weary people wonder if, indeed, the news is good. There are times when the teacher is needed to clarify issues and remind us of the Church's tradition, especially when that tradition is misunderstood or misrepresented. There are times, also, to hear the witness who is called forth to testify to Christ in the world. And there is always the time when the voice of the interpreter needs to be heard, a strong poetic and prophetic voice that helps to unravel our thoughts and penetrate our hearts so that the gospel can be heard again.

Notes

1. Avery Dulles, S.J., *Models of the Church: A Critical Assessment of the Church in All Its Aspects* (Garden City, N.Y.: Doubleday, 1974) 8.

2. Thomas G. Long, *The Witness of Preaching* (Louisville: Westminster/John Knox Press, 1989) 24.

3. See also James A. Wallace, C.Ss.R., *Imaginal Preaching* (New York: Paulist Press, 1995) 10–5.

4. Some of this material was covered in my article "Heralds of Hope" in *Liturgy 90* (August/September 1996) 4–7, 14.

5. See Josef Andreas Jungmann, S.J., *The Good News Yesterday and Today*, trans. William Huesman, S.J. (New York: Sadlier, 1962).

6. Josef A. Jungmann, S.J., *Announcing the Word of God*, trans. Ronald Walls (New York: Herder and Herder, 1967) 59.

7. William O'Shea, S.S., "The Sermon is Part of the Mass," *The Homiletic and Pastoral Review* (March 1960) 519.

8. Karl Rahner, S.J., "Kerygmatische Theologie" in *Lexikon für Theologie und Kirche,* ed. Josef Hofer and Karl Rahner (Frieburg: Herder, 1966) 136.

9. Martin Luther, *Winkelmesse und Pfaffenweihe,* 1553 as quoted in Henry Grady Davis, *Design for Preaching* (Philadelphia: Fortress Press, 1958) 120.

10. Robert F. McNamara, *Catholic Sunday Preaching: The American Guidelines 1791–1975* (Washington, D.C.: Word of God Institute, 1975).

11. Ibid., 25–6.

12. Congregation For The Clergy, *Directory on the Ministry and Life of Priests* (Roma: Libreria Editrice Vaticana, 1994) 47.

13. Edward Schillebeeckx, O.P., *Church: the Human Story of God* (New York: Crossroad, 1991) 40–1.

14. Mary Catherine Hilkert, O.P., "Revelation and Proclamation: Shifting Paradigms," *In the Company of Preachers,* Aquinas Institute of Theology Faculty (Collegeville: The Liturgical Press, 1993) 127.

15. William A. Richard, "Preaching the Dark Side of the Gospel," *Worship* (March 1987) 12.

16. Raymond E. Brown, S.S., *A Coming of Christ in Advent* (Collegeville: The Liturgical Press, 1988) 12.

17. Pope Paul VI, *On Evangelization in the Modern World* (Washington, D.C.: United States Catholic Conference, 1976) 29.

18. Walter J. Burghardt, S.J., *Preaching: The Art and the Craft* (New York: Paulist Press, 1987) 10.

19. Pope John Paul II, *Catechesi tradendae,* 16 October 1979, AAS 71 (Vatican City: Vatican Polyglot Press, 1979) 48.

20. Saint Augustine, *On Christian Doctrine,* trans. D. W. Robertson, Jr. (New York: Liberal Arts Press, 1978) 141.

21. Joseph Fichtner, O.S.C., *To Stand and Speak for Christ* (New York: Alba House, 1981) 82.

22. Burghardt, *Preaching,* 9.

23. C. H. Dodd, *The Apostolic Preaching and Its Developments* (London: Holder and Stoughton, 1963).

24. Fichtner, *To Stand and Speak for Christ,* 88.

25. Willard Francis Jabusch, *The Spoken Christ: Reading and Preaching the Transforming Word* (New York: Crossroad, 1990) 45.

26. Lawrence E. Mick, *RCIA: Renewing the Church as an Initiating Assembly* (Collegeville: The Liturgical Press, 1989) 17.

27. See E. J. Tinsley, "Mystery religions" in *The Westminster Dictionary of Christian Theology,* Alan Richardson and John Bowden, eds. (Philadelphia: The Westminster Press, 1983) 386. See also Edward Yarnold, S.J., *The Awe-Inspiring Rites of Initiation: The Origins of the RCIA* (Collegeville: The Liturgical Press, 1994) 59–66. Yarnold holds that the rites of initiation were hardly influenced by the pagan mystery religions but that "the explanation given of them began to emphasize the element of mystery and fear" (66).

28. Enrico Mazza, *Mystagogy* (New York: Pueblo Publishing, 1989; Collegeville: The Liturgical Press, 1990) x.

29. Alan of Lille, *The Art of Preaching* Cistercian Fathers Series, no 23, trans. Gilian R. Evans (Kalamazoo: Cistercian Publications, 1981), 17.

30. Dom Gregory Dix, O.S.B., *The Shape of the Liturgy* (New York: Seabury Press, 1982) 596–7.

31. J. Kevin Coyle, "From Homily to Sermon to Homily: The Content of Christian Preaching in Historical Perspective," *Liturgical Ministry* (Winter 1992) 8.

32. See Robert P. Waznak, S.S., "The Catechism and the Sunday Homily," *America* (October 22, 1994) 18–21.

33. See the research and insights of Stephen V. DeLeers, "Written Text Becomes Living Word": Official Roman Catholic Teaching on the Homily, 1963–1993, *Papers for the 1996 Meeting of the Academy of Homiletics,* Santa Fe, N.M. (December 1996) 4.

34. Paul VI, *On Evangelization in the Modern World,* 43.

35. John Paul II, *Catechesi tradendae,* 48.

36. *Catechism of the Catholic Church* (Liguori, Mo.: Liturgical Publications, 1994) #2033.

37. Gerard S. Sloyan, "The Homily and Catechesis: The Catechism and/or the Lectionary?" *Introducing the Catechism of the Catholic Church,* ed. Berard L. Marthaler, O.F.M., Conv. (New York: Paulist Press, 1994) 141.

38. Charles E. Miller, C.M., *Ordained to Preach* (New York: Alba House 1992) 109.

39. Samuel E. Torvend, "Preaching the Liturgy: A Social Mystagogy," *In the Company of Preachers,* Aquinas Institute of Theology Faculty, 52.

40. Daniel Patte, *Preaching Paul* (Philadelphia: Fortress Press, 1984) 60–1.

41. Sloyan, "The Homily and Catechesis," 138.

42. Gerard S. Sloyan, "Is Church Teaching Neglected When the Lectionary Is Preached?" *Worship* (March 1987) 126.

43. Ibid., 139.

44. Jabusch, *The Spoken Christ,* 43.

45. Saint Augustine, *On Christian Doctrine,* trans. D. W. Robertson, Jr. 4. 17.34, 142.

46. See Frederick J. McGinness, *Right Thinking and Sacred Oratory in Counter-Reformation Rome* (Princeton, N.J.: Princeton University Press, 1995) 55.

47. Aristotle, *Rhetoric,* Book I, chapter 3, trans. W. Rhys Roberts (New York: Modern Library, 1954) 31–2.

48. John W. O'Malley, S.J., *Praise and Blame in Renaissance Rome: Rhetoric, Doctrine, and Reform in the Sacred Orators of the Papal Court, c. 1440–1521* (Durham: N.C.: Duke University Press, 1979).

49. See James M. Schmitmeyer, "Literature, Homiletics and the Absence of God" *Worship* (January 1989) 48–65.

50. Lawrence W. Rosenfield, "The Practical Celebration of Epideictic," *Rhetoric in Transition,* ed. Eugene White (University Park: Pennsylvania State University Press, 1980) 131–55.

51. Schmitmeyer, "Literature, Homiletics and the Absence of God," 49.

52. David Buttrick, *Homiletic: Moves and Structures* (Philadelphia: Fortress Press, 1987) 8.

53. Mary Catherine Hilkert, O.P., *Naming Grace: Preaching and the Sacramental Imagination* (New York: Continuum, 1997).

54. Yngve Brilioth, *A Brief History of Preaching* (Philadelphia: Fortress Press, 1965) 8–10.

55. Aidan Kavanagh, *On Liturgical Theology* (New York: Pueblo Publishing Company, 1984; Collegeville: The Liturgical Press, 1990) 82.

56. James A. Wallace, C.Ss.R., "Guidelines for Preaching by the Laity: Another Step Backward?" *America* (September 9–16, 1989) 140.

57. David Tracy, *Blessed Rage for Order: The New Pluralism in Theology* (New York: Seabury Press, 1975) 43.

58. Hilkert, *Naming Grace,* 34.

59. Michael Skelley, S.J., "The Liturgy of the World and the Liturgy of the Church: Karl Rahner's Idea of Worship," *Worship* (March 1989) 125.

60. Michael Skelley, S.J., *The Liturgy of the World: Karl Rahner's Theology of Worship* (Collegeville: The Liturgical Press, 1991) 75.

61. Karl Rahner, S.J., ed., *The Renewal of Preaching: Theory and Practice,* trans. Theodore L. Westow (New York: Paulist Press, 1968) 1.

62. David Buttrick, *A Captive Voice: The Liberation of Preaching* (Louisville: Westminster/John Knox Press, 1994) 110.

63. Fred B. Craddock, *As One Without Authority* (Nashville: Abingdon Press, 1971) 9. Also see Robert P. Waznak, S.S., "Preaching the Gospel in a Video Culture" in *Media, Culture, and Catholicism,* ed. Paul A. Soukup (Kansas City, Mo.: Sheed & Ward, 1996) 133–43.

64. Gerard S. Sloyan, *Worshipful Preaching* (Philadelphia: Fortress Press, 1984) 57.

65. Karl Rahner, S.J., "Priest and Poet," *The Word: Readings in Theology,* trans. Carney Gavin (New York: P. J. Kenedy and Sons, 1964) 24.

66. Buttrick, *Homiletic,* 189.

67. As quoted in Fred B. Craddock, *Overhearing the Gospel* (Nashville: Abingdon Press, 1978) 9.

68. Burghardt, *Preaching,* 34.

69. Elizabeth Barrett Browning, "Aurora Leigh," *The Poetical Works of Elizabeth Barrett Browning* (New York: MacMillan, 1987) 466.

70. As recorded in the First Canonization Enquiry of Saint Thomas Aquinas. See Kenelm Foster, O.P., ed. and trans., *The Life of Saint Thomas Aquinas* (Baltimore: Helicon Press, 1959) 110.

71. St. Thomas Aquinas, *Summa Theologica,* II–II, q. 188, a. 7.

72. John Francis Kavanaugh, *Following Christ in a Consumer Society: The Spiritual Cultural Resistance* (Maryknoll, N.Y.: Orbis Books, 1982) 56.

73. Robert Bellah et al, *Habits of the Heart: Individualism and Commitment in American Life* (Berkeley: University of California Press, 1985) 37.

74. See T. Howland Sanks, S.J., *Salt, Leaven, and Light* (New York: Crossroad, 1992) 3–22.

75. See Dean Hoge, *Converts, Dropouts, Returnees: A Study of Religious Change Among Catholics* (New York: Pilgrim Press, 1981) and Jim Casteli and Joseph Gremillion, *The Emerging Parish: The Notre Dame Study of Catholic Life Since Vatican II* (San Francisco: Harper & Row, 1987).

76. Buttrick, *A Captive Voice,* 72.

77. Karl Barth, *Homiletics,* trans. Geoffrey W. Bromiley and Donald E. Daniels (Louisville: Westminster/John Knox Press, 1991) 119.

78. Karl Barth, *The Preaching of the Gospel,* trans. B. E. Hooke (Philadelphia: Westminster Press, 1993) 43.

79. Barth, *Homiletics,* 118–9.

80. Walter Brueggemann, *Finally Comes the Poet: Daring Speech for Proclamation* (Minneapolis: Fortress Press, 1989) 6.

81. Burghardt, *Preaching,* 131.

82. Paul Scott Wilson, *Imagination of the Heart: New Understandings in Preaching* (Nashville: Abingdon Press, 1988) 198.

83. Brueggemann, *Finally Comes the Poet,* 109–10.

84. Pope John Paul II, homily preached at Santo Domingo's Independence Plaza, January 25, 1979 in *Origins* (February 8, 1979) 543.

85. Jean Delumeau, *Sin and Fear: The Emergence of a Western Guilt Culture 13th–18th Centuries,* trans. Eric Nicholson (New York: St. Martin's Press, 1990).

86. Walter Brueggemann, *The Bible Makes Sense* (Winona, Minn.: St. Mary's College Press, 1978) 12.

87. Bill C. Davis, *Mass Appeal* (New York: Dramatists Play Service, Inc. 1981) 18, 19, 51.

88. Pope Paul VI, *On Evangelization In the Modern World,* 76.

89. Ibid., 41, 76.

90. Richard L. Thulin, *The "I" Of The Sermon* (Minneapolis: Fortress Press, 1989).

91. Buttrick, *Homiletic,* 142.

92. Catherine Mowry LaCugna, "Reflections on Preaching the Word of God," *America* (March 19–26, 1994) 4.

93. Hilkert, *Naming Grace,* 16.

94. Walter J. Burghardt, S.J., *Seasons That Laugh or Weep* (New York: Paulist Press, 1983) 77.

95. Ronald D. Witherup, S.S., *Conversion in the New Testament* (Collegeville: The Liturgical Press, 1994) 83.

96. William Sloane Coffin, *The Courage to Love* (San Francisco: Harper & Row, 1982) 9.

97. Thulin, *The "I" of the Sermon,* 14.

98. Richard A. Jensen, *Telling the Story* (Minneapolis: Augsburg, 1980) 152.

99. Robert P. Waznak, S.S., *Like Fresh Bread: Sunday Homilies in the Parish* (New York: Paulist Press, 1993) 21–2.

100. John Killenger, *Fundamentals of Preaching* (Philadelphia: Fortress Press, 1985) 31.

101. Elie Wiesel, *The Messengers of God: Biblical Portraits and Legends,* trans. Marion Wiesel (New York: Pocket Books, 1977) 12.

102. See Robert P. Waznak, S.S., *Sunday After Sunday: Preaching the Homily as Story* (New York: Paulist Press, 1983).

103. *Directory on the Ministry and Life of Priests,* 35.

104. Ibid., 47.

3

The Lectionary: Richer Fare or Lesser Choice?

An introductory text on the homily must by necessity examine the homilist's handbook, the Lectionary. In homily preparation preachers are constantly making decisions about content and form. Homilists who lack a proper understanding of the purpose and the plan of the Lectionary often make decisions that rob the homily of clarity, focus, and liturgical intention. What follows is a brief historical overview and an explication of the purpose and the plan of the Lectionary with accompanying caveats and suggestions to help assist the preacher in homiletic decision making.

The preaching that prevailed during the time immediately before the Second Vatican Council was often based on outlines of doctrinal topics with little or no reference to the biblical texts of the liturgy. A good deal of Catholic preaching prior to the council amounted to not much more than a retelling of the gospel story with moral exhortations. Lacking an authentic biblical foundation, most sermons were about God's concern for the "salvation of souls." Scripture texts were used to back up what the priest was trying to teach (known as "proof-texting"). The parables of Jesus were often presented as allegories about sanctifying grace rather than startling images of God's reign. The miracles of Jesus were preached as proofs of his divinity rather than signs of the reign of God. The Old Testament, if it was preached, was viewed as something old indeed. Pious proverbs and moral exhortations were drawn from those ancient books. The "unfaithful" Jews of the Hebrew Scriptures were often presented as foils for the faithful disciples of the New Testament.

But then came the Second Vatican Council where the fruits of biblical scholarship encouraged by Pope Pius XII's breakthrough encyclical *Divino Afflante Spiritu* (1943) found their way into all sixteen documents of the council. The first ritual that occurred at the opening of Vatican II was the enshrinement of the Holy Scriptures.

The council made some revolutionary statements about a return to the biblical proclamation of the early Church:

> It follows that all the preaching of the Church, as indeed the entire Christian religion, should be nourished and ruled by Sacred Scripture (*DV*, 21).

> Sacred scripture is of the greatest importance in the celebration of the liturgy (*SC*, 24).

> The sermon, moreover, should draw its content mainly from scriptural and liturgical sources (*SC*, 35).

> The treasures of the Bible are to be opened up more lavishly so that a richer fare may be provided for the faithful at the table of God's word. In this way a more suitable part of the sacred scriptures will be read to the people in the course of a prescribed number of years (*SC*, 51).

If the homily was to be restored to its biblical and liturgical foundations, something had to be done about assuring that more of the Bible was proclaimed in liturgical celebrations. Prior to the council there was a one-year cycle of readings (epistles and gospels) that had been in place since the *Missale Romanum* of 1570. The council's call for a "richer fare" of the Bible led to the formulation of a new Lectionary with a three-year cycle of readings.

History of the Lectionary

A lectionary is an "orderly sequence of selections from Scripture to be read aloud at public worship by a religious community."[1] Lectionaries serve to give uniformity to worship and to provide continuity from one generation to the next. They challenge the subjectivity of the preacher content to ride the same hobbyhorse each Sunday with "favorite scripture passages." There is always the danger that the Bible can be used against people rather than for them. One should be wary of the preacher who begins a homily by saying, "I have selected this passage from Scripture because it means so much to me, and I hope it will for you." John Calvin, who abolished the classic order of the church year, nevertheless advocated the practice of *lectio continua* (the systematic public reading of the books of the Bible each Sunday) "so that the church would not be subjected to the momentary whims of the preacher."[2] Preaching from lectionaries preserves the image of the homilist as a servant of the word of God who first listens and broods over the biblical lessons before preaching them to others.

The tradition of planning a set of readings from Scripture has its roots in ancient Jewish synagogue ritual when the Torah was read as a first reading and an excerpt from the Prophets *(haftarah)* was read to explicate the Torah text of the day. There are some scholars who believe that the gospels themselves reveal a series of liturgical pericopes (from the Greek word which means a selection "cut around"). A few authors suggest that when Jesus said, "Today this scripture has been fulfilled in your hearing" (Luke 4:21), the scripture (Isa 61) was a prescribed passage which had been marked in the scroll by the archisynagogus from the prophetic cycle of readings. As early as the fourth century in *The Apostolic Constitutions,* there is reference to "reading of the law and the prophets, of our epistles and the Acts, as well as the Gospels, a five-lesson sequence."[3]

The council's call for a "richer fare" of scripture readings led to a new Lectionary. It was the work of the *Coetus XI,* one of the dozen study groups of the *Consilium,* a commission designed to implement Vatican II's liturgical reforms. Godfrey Diekmann of St. John's Abbey, Collegeville, Minnesota, was the relator of *Coetus XI.* Diekmann set forth the Lectionary's basic principle:

> "[T]he mystery of Christ and the history of salvation" must be presented in the readings. Therefore, the new system of readings must contain the nucleus of the apostolic preaching about Jesus as "Lord and Christ" (Acts 2:36) who fulfilled the Scriptures by his life, his preaching, and, above all, his paschal mystery and who gives life to the Church until his glorious return.[4]

This basic principle which emphasized the paschal mystery of Christ prevailed despite the calls in some circles that the Lectionary be formulated to present a systematic treatment of the teachings of the Church.

The eighteen members of the special commission on the Lectionary extensively researched lectionaries, both ancient and modern, Eastern and Western, used both in the Catholic and non-Catholic communities. They asked thirty-one biblical scholars to select from all the books of the Bible passages that they regarded as best suited for liturgical use. The scholars' list was then sent to a hundred catechetical experts or pastors for their feedback. Finally, *The Revised Lectionary of the Roman Missal for Sundays and Solemnities* was published by the Congregation for Divine Worship on May 25, 1969. It was authorized for use in the dioceses of the United States by the National Conference of Catholic Bishops beginning Palm Sunday 1970 and was made mandatory beginning the first Sunday of Advent 1971. A two-year weekday Lectionary accompanied the new three-year cycle of readings. The *Missale Romanum* of 1570 contained about 5 percent of the Bible—1 percent of the Old Testament and 16 percent of the New. The new Lectionary contains approximately 13 percent of the Bible—6 percent of the Old Testament (not counting the Psalms) and 41 percent of the New.[5] Thus, the Lectionary does offer *more* of the Bible but not *all* of the Bible.

The Roman Lectionary had widespread ecumenical appeal and was adopted with necessary denominational revisions by the Episcopal Church (1970) and various Protestant denominations including Presbyterians (1970) and Lutherans (1973). In 1983, a group of denominations produced a *Common Lectionary* that was also based on the Roman Lectionary. However, the framers of the *Common Lectionary* chose Old Testament semi-continuous readings during much of Ordinary Time, to provide week-to-week continuity in Hebrew scripture. To avoid typological principles, during the Year A, readings from Torah were used, since Matthew is the most "Jewish" of the Gospels. Mark's interest in the title "Son of David" dictated Davidic narratives for Year B. Luke's concern for social justice led to the use of the Hebrew prophets during Year C. The framers of the *Common Lectionary* followed the Episcopal Lectionary by providing alternate readings to the deuterocanonical books on the days the Roman Lectionary proposes them as the only reading. Presbyterians, United Church of Christ, Disciples of Christ, United Methodists, and Lutherans follow the *Common Lectionary* that was revised in 1992. The *Revised Common Lectionary,* like its predecessor, made provision for paired readings in which the first and gospel readings are closely related (during Advent, Christmas, Lent, and Easter) and for semi-continuous Old Testament readings during Ordinary Time. Some Catholic authors have advocated abandoning the Roman Lectionary in favor of the Common.[6]

The 1993 document of the Pontifical Biblical Commission, The Interpretation of the Bible in the Church, hints at the possibility of a revision of the current Roman Lectionary. Commenting on Vatican II's goal of a lectionary with more abundant, varied, and suitable representation of the Bible, the document states that the Lectionary "in its present state . . . only partially fulfills this goal."[7]

The Roman Lectionary is a product of its time. When it was composed, literary-critical methods of biblical interpretation "which might have influenced the selection, delimitation, and distribution of scriptural passages, had yet to make their appearance."[8] The members of *Coetus XI* were all men, the majority from Europe, with only two representatives from North America and none from other continents. Feminist hermeneutics had not yet made its mark. The PBC document now recognizes that feminist hermeneutics help "unmask and correct certain commonly accepted interpretations which were tendentious and sought to justify the male domination of women."[9]

Structure of the Lectionary

There are some preachers whose homilies consist of the format: "In the first reading we hear, in the second reading we have, in the third reading we find." In forcing a common theme on all three readings, homilists often miss the major theme of one or more of the readings and "with considerable ingenuity, find a strained connection by means of minor emphasis or incidentals."[10] Besides being a boring and predictable pattern, such homilies demonstrate a lack of understanding of how and why the lectionary readings were structured. A review of that structure is in order.

In the Roman Lectionary three readings are assigned to every Sunday of the liturgical year according to a three-year cycle. The first reading is taken from the Old Testament (its place is substituted by Acts in Eastertide), the second from the apostolic writings (either from a letter or from Revelation, depending on the season), and the third from the gospels. A responsorial psalm is meant to be a sung response to the first reading; an acclamation precedes the proclamation of the gospel.

For most of the year, the gospel pericopes are semi-continuous from a book in its chapter sequence. The Old Testament readings do not manifest any such sequence since they were selected to correspond with the gospel readings in order to demonstrate "the unity of the Old and New Testaments and of the history of salvation, in which Christ is the central figure, commemorated in his paschal mystery."[11]

This process of harmonization is also known as the typological principle since something in the Old Testament is found to be a *typos* (model or example) of an event in the life of Jesus. The typological principle was often employed by the early Church Fathers.

During Ordinary Time, the second reading is not meant to harmonize with the other two readings. The second reading follows a semi-continuous pattern. The one exception to this pattern is the reading of First Corinthians and the Letter to the Hebrews over three years. For the Sundays of Advent, Christmas, Lent, and Eastertide and also for major feast days of the sanctoral cycle, the three readings do reflect a unity of theme since they were chosen to fit the themes of the feast or the season. The readings of the major liturgical seasons were chosen from tradition, e.g., Isaiah in Advent, John's Gospel in Lent and Eastertide, the Acts of the Apostles at Eastertide, and special gospel readings on the third, fourth, and fifth Sunday of Lent because of the liturgical scrutinies of the RCIA (Rite of Christian Initiation of Adults) celebrated on those Sundays. Therefore, except for the seasons of Advent, Lent, Eastertide, and the principal feasts, the three readings do not evidence a unity of theme. The compilers of the Lectionary were not concerned with the thematic interrelationship of the readings but with a tract that provided the assembly with as much of the Bible as possible and which focused on the paschal mystery of Christ. The *Lectionary for Mass: General Instruction* states:

> The decision was made not to extend to Sundays the arrangement suited to the liturgical seasons mentioned, that is, not to have an organic harmony of single themes designed to aid homiletic instruction. Such an arrangement would be in conflict with the genuine conception of liturgical celebration. The liturgy is always the celebration of the mystery of Christ and makes use of the word of God on the basis of its own tradition, guided not by merely logical or extrinsic concerns but by the desire to proclaim the gospel and to lead those who believe to the fullness of the truth.[12]

The essential characteristic which differentiates each year from another is the gospel which is read as the principal lesson: Year A, Matthew; Year B, Mark; Year C, Luke. Because Mark is shorter than the other synoptics, it is complemented with readings from John. The Fourth Gospel is allotted its traditional privileged position through the cycle, i.e., it is read on many of the Sundays of Lent and Easter.

Modern biblical research, particularly redaction criticism, played a role in the decision to assign one synoptic gospel to each year of a three-year cycle. Thus, the uniqueness of each synoptic gospel's presentation of the story of Jesus is highlighted. Homilists, therefore, can and should draw upon this uniqueness in the preparation of their homilies.

Two weekday readings are assigned to the two-year weekday Lectionary. The first is from the Old Testament or from an apostle (from a letter or from Revelation), and during Eastertide from Acts; the second reading is from the Gospels. The gospel pericopes are arranged in a single cycle, repeated each year. The first reading, however, is arranged in a two-year cycle and is thus read every other year. The weekday readings are governed by the semi-continuous principle. There is, therefore, a random relationship between the two readings in either year except in the seasons which have their own distinctive character. There is a yearly cycle of readings during Lent, Advent, Christmas, and Eastertide. The readings of Lent take into account the baptismal and penitential themes of the season.

The readings of the feasts of the Lord, of Mary, and the Feasts and Solemnities of the saints were chosen to fit the event or the saint celebrated. Under the headings "Ritual Masses" and "Masses for Various Occasions," the Lectionary also lists a series of readings for various sacramental rites (baptism, marriage, funeral), for specific groups (refugees and exiles), and intentions (peace and justice). The pastoral needs of the particular liturgical assembly should determine the choice of readings.

Problems and Suggestions

The Roman Lectionary has made a significant contribution to the life and preaching of the Church. More and varied readings and an opportunity to emphasize the character and theology of each of the evangelists have helped shape our preaching. Methodist scholar James White describes the Roman Lectionary as "Catholicism's greatest gift to Protestant preaching."[13] This does not mean that the Lectionary is perfect nor does it mean that it does not pose problems for homilists. Liturgical scholars and preachers in the field have had their fair share of complaints about the Lectionary. What follows is a catalogue of those complaints with an attempt to provide some practical suggestions to the problems raised.

1) *Difficulty of preaching on three readings*

In 1964 Godfrey Diekmann suggested to the group composing the new Lectionary that of the three readings, the first or the second should be optional. He may have been attempting to be sensitive to some who were complaining that Catholics were not accustomed to listen to a lengthy Liturgy of the Word. But in 1966 it was decided to accept the three readings as obligatory. The decision came with a proviso that for "pastoral reasons" a conference of bishops could decide on permitting two instead of three readings. It should be noted that when this occurs, it is not the Old Testament reading that is omitted.[14] Some of the reasons for the decision to have three readings were to fulfill Vatican II's desire that a "richer fare" of the Scriptures be read to people; a return to the early traditions found in Augustine, Ambrose, and still found in various liturgies such as the Ambrosian and Gallican; to demonstrate "the unity of the two Testaments and of the entire history of salvation."[15]

Despite these lofty reasons, preachers were left with some practical decisions about how to attend to the three lessons in a Sunday homily. Vatican II stated that the Scripture "lessons" (plural) are "explained in the homily" (*SC,* 24). How can a homilist explain the readings in the short time allotted for the homily? In a future revision of the Lectionary, Gerard Sloyan has proposed a two-reading structure where the Old Testament reading or the epistle is lengthened:

> There *are* too many to come at any hearer profitably, even given a good rhythm of pacing and an excellent homily. Less is truly more. But "less" here means fewer, not briefer. The first, non-gospel reading has to be extensive, letting biblical authors have their full say. Only then will hearers be instructed and homilists be impelled to preach.[16]

In the meantime some authors have offered practical suggestions to deal with the three-reading structure as it now exists. O. C. Edwards, Jr., believes that "the homily should begin with the gospel and bring in the other lessons only if they are serendipitous." Edwards offers that advice because he believes that it is difficult "to make one point clearly in the time available for the homily."[17] Paul Scott Wilson asserts that "not every text read in worship *can* be treated in the sermon or homily, at least with the attention that it deserves and we deserve . . . that means choosing a primary text and giving more than just a sporting chance for its music to be heard."[18]

The compilers of the Lectionary selected the gospel lesson as the controlling reading for the Liturgy of the Word in Ordinary Time: "The reading of the gospel is the high point of the liturgy of the word. For this the other readings, in their established sequence from the Old to the New Testament, prepare the assembly."[19] This follows an ancient liturgical tradition where the gospel was given primacy of place as evidenced by its position of honor as last in the sequence of readings, proclaimed by an ordained minister from a bejeweled book, and surrounded with symbols of honor: lights, incense, and kisses. William Skudlarek believes that the "prestigious position of the Gospel in the liturgy, as well as the relative familiarity and accessibility of the Gospel passages, predisposes and prepares a congregation for preaching which is more closely related to it than to the other scriptural lessons."[20]

Although Skudlarek believes that the gospel lesson will normally be the principal scriptural source for the homily and that the homilist need not refer to all three readings and the psalm in the homily, he advises the homilist to study all three lessons not for the purpose of tying them all together but in order "to establish a hermeneutical dialogue among themselves."[21] Since the Old Testament reading was selected to harmonize with the gospel reading, this hermeneutical dialogue will be fairly predictable. But Skudlarek believes that the dialogue can occur also with the second reading even though it is not thematically related to the other two lessons. "The very fact that it is unrelated is what makes the textual dialogue such a powerful source for creative insight."[22]

For example, on the Twenty-Third Sunday of the Year (C), in the first reading (Wis 9:13-18), we hear the biblical author place a prayer for wisdom on the lips of Israel's paragon of wisdom, King Solomon, who says that "the reasoning of mortals is worthless"; they need the counsel of "your holy spirit from on high." In the second lesson (Phlm 9–10, 12–17), St. Paul pleads with Philemon to take back his former slave Onesimus not as a slave but as "a beloved brother." In the gospel reading (Luke 14:25-33), we hear the evangelist's account of Jesus turning to a great crowd following him and telling the people if they do not take up the cross and follow him they cannot be his disciples. This is followed by two parables about how people must sit down and calculate the cost before they begin a project. The homilist may wish to focus on the need to seek the wisdom of the Holy Spirit before making important decisions in life (first and third reading) or may wish to highlight the cost of discipleship (second and third reading). What will determine the homilist's choice is the particular interpretation of life that is given because of the concrete circumstances of those gathered to celebrate the paschal mystery of Christ.

Skudlarek's homiletic advice preserves two important principles. First, it values an imaginative dwelling with the Scripture readings. Creative homilies spring not from a slavish attempt to explain all three lessons but from a prayerful and imaginative dwelling with all of the readings of a particular liturgy. The question, therefore, is not how much of Scripture can be digested by the faithful but how creative juxtapositions of the readings can shed new light and breathe fresh spirit on their lives. Creative preachers see relationships between biblical lessons, a pericope and a current event, theology and life, that others often miss. Henri Poincaré wrote of making combinations that "reveal to us unexpected kinship between facts long known but wrongly believed to be strangers to one another."[23]

Secondly, Skudlarek's advice reminds us that "the preacher does not so much attempt to explain the Scriptures as to interpret the human situation through the Scriptures" (*FIYH*, 20). The liturgical calendar and the people's calendar do not always interlink. Certain situations arise—a secular holiday, a national or international tragic event, a church controversy, a particular pastoral need to hear a Pauline doctrine. These situations do not necessarily dovetail with the gospel lesson of the day. Since the homily is not just an interpretation of the biblical texts but of human existence, a preacher dare not ignore the people's calendar. There will be times when the events, characters, mystery, advice, images, and metaphors in the second reading and/or the Old Testament lesson or a creative interplay between one or two of the lessons with the gospel reading will open fresh possibilities for a scriptural interpretation of a particular life situation. It would not be appropriate, however, to the purposes of the Lectionary and the liturgical year to skip the gospel Sunday after Sunday in favor of one of the other two lessons.

2) *The Psalm Response*

The *Lectionary for Mass* makes it clear that "the psalm after the first reading is very important" (89). Some liturgists have argued that this psalm deserves attention as a source of preaching. Jan Michael Joncas believes that "we have understood the adjective 'responsorial' as a functional description rather than a musical one."[24] He makes a case that the psalm is a sung proclamation of the word of God and not a "meditation song." Joncas has liturgical tradition to rely upon. He points to a homily on Psalm 130/131 by the fourth-century bishop of Poitiers, Hilary. One could also point to the description of the homily in the General Instruction of the Roman Missal (41): "It should develop some point of the readings *or of another text from the Ordinary or from the Proper of the Mass of the day*" (emphasis mine).

In mystagogical preaching, especially aimed at neophytes in the RCIA, the psalm or another text from the Ordinary or from the Proper of the Mass of the day can provide homilists with a rich resource. St. Augustine preached on the "Lift up your hearts" on several occasions in order to draw attention to its deeper significance. The psalms and texts of the Mass other than the three readings are rich in imagery and speak to our spiritual yearnings.

But it is clear from #318 of the General Instruction that "Sundays and holydays have *three* readings, that is, from the Old Testament, from the writings of an apostle, and from a Gospel" (emphasis mine). The psalm after the first reading is not another reading. But while meditating on the three Sunday readings, homilists should also keep their sights on the psalm response as well as the prayers of the liturgy of the day for further meaning and unexpected insights into the three readings. Irene Nowell advises preachers to "play with the readings. Play with the images, with the interrelationships. Sing the psalm in different voices. Explore the contradictions. Enjoy the rich weave of the whole Liturgy of the Word."[25]

3) *The Second Reading*

Because the second reading on a Sunday in Ordinary Time is not meant to harmonize with the other two lessons, it does cause problems for hearers and preachers. It is like watching your favorite television program and at the same time trying to read the warnings of a hurricane that flash on the bottom of the television screen. Or it is similar to an orchestra beginning with an overture to *Romeo and Juliet* (Old Testament reading), then switching to the music of *Hello Dolly* (second reading), and finally ending with the music of *West Side Story* (gospel reading). One could discern the connection between *Romeo and Juliet* and *West Side Story*, but *Hello Dolly* in the middle of the common theme of star-crossed lovers is confusing and jolting. In a future revision of the Lectionary, some liturgists have proposed that the second lesson be read at the end of the liturgy as a dismissal, similar to the *haftarah* at the end of the ancient synagogue service.

In the meantime, there are some practical choices a homilist can make regarding the second reading. First, a homilist does not have to refer to the second reading in the homily. Most of the letters of Paul or his disciples that we hear at Mass are hortatory in tone. They do not need elaboration or doctrinal stress. If they are proclaimed well, the exhortation will be heard by the assembly. Second, as was mentioned above, the second reading might speak on a particular Sunday more existentially to the congregation than the gospel lesson because of some parochial, national, international event, or pastoral need. The perceptive preacher who reads the signs of the times should not dismiss the possibilities of the second reading. Two splendid preaching resources for employing Pauline texts in preaching are Daniel Patte's *Preaching Paul* and Raymond Collins' *Preaching the Epistles*.[26]

4) *Devaluation of the Old Testament*

Since the gospel pericope sets the theme for the liturgical calendar, the choice of the Old Testament reading was made solely for the purpose of harmonization. This could lead some homilists to develop a hermeneutic of evolutionism—the anti-Semitic hermeneutic which holds that what is later in the Bible is somehow better. Contemporary authors in intertestamental studies point to the inadequacy of the assumption that the Old Testament is "fulfilled" in the New Testament. These biblical scholars demonstrate how the evangelists often modified and wove Old Testament traditions into the gospels for their own hermeneutical reasons. Gerard Sloyan warns against the fulfillment principle of interpretation where Jews are portrayed as incomplete, disloyal, and condemned, while the disciples are justified in Jesus:

> It might be called "realized eschatology with a vengeance." This is the triumphal understanding that all that has been realized in the Christ of glory has been realized in Christians. Since lectionary choices can contribute to this mentality, it must be all the more vigilantly resisted when they are employed.[27]

Because the Old Testament was chosen to harmonize with the gospel reading, we often hear mere snippets of the first reading rather than enjoy them as integral stories in their own context.[28] Sloyan laments that we "hear, not the great stories of the Bible as history, but the First Testament trained as a very weak torch-beam on the Second."[29]

Gail Ramshaw has pointed out that while Christians cannot avoid using the First Testament in a distinctively Christian way toward distinctively Christian meaning, "we must halt an anti-Semitic replacement theology."[30] She suggests that Christian homilists employ the metaphors of the Old Testament to enrich their understanding of the gospel readings. For example, the Old Testament readings at the Easter Vigil about the creation of the world, Noah saved from the flood, Isaac saved from the knife, and the Israelites saved from Pharoah's army are all "metaphoric ways Christians celebrate the resurrection."[31] Ramshaw's suggestion is in concert with Sloyan's reminder that the "oldest principle of biblical interpretation" is one where "later verbal symbols throw light on earlier ones in a cascade of imagery that conveys some sense of the divine."[32]

5) *The exclusivity of the Lectionary*

Because the Old Testament readings were selected to harmonize with the gospel lessons, many of the great themes of the Bible are left out of the Lectionary. The image or word hopping methodology of the Lectionary (a storm in the gospel is lined up to a storm in the Old Testament) often slights the original context and meaning of an Old Testament theme. The theme of God's grandeur of creation is heard only at the Easter Vigil. The Lectionary does not highlight the pathos of human life that is found in Job or in the Psalms. The great moral tales (e.g., the story of David's relationship with Nabal and Abigail) that help the hearer wrestle with human dilemmas are often ignored and substituted for exhortations to virtue such as those found in the Book of Proverbs.

Operating with their "hermeneutic of suspicion" liberation theologians are critical of the fact that much of the struggle between the powerful and the powerless from the Old Testament is missing in the Lectionary.[33] While there are many selections from Deuteronomy and Leviticus, the more radical views of these two books are not presented: that the land belongs to God and cannot be held forever by anyone; at the time of jubilee, there shall be a general release from creditors. There is a short snippet from the prophet Micah found on the Fourth Sunday of Advent (C). It is chosen because of its reference to Bethlehem as the birthplace of the ruler of Israel. But the Lectionary never presents the prophet's message of a new order of peace and justice.

Feminist authors have been particularly critical of the exclusion of many biblical women. They believe that the Lectionary selections have actually heightened the androcentrism of the Bible. Marjorie Procter-Smith writes:

> While biblical texts themselves generally present women as adjuncts to men, the lectionary hermeneutic, by intention to be selective, and by its tendency to focus on a few central major figures, such as Moses, David and Elijah, or the male disciples of Jesus (especially Peter and Paul), increase this marginalization of women characters.[34]

On the Thirty-Third Sunday of the Year (A), we hear about the worthy wife from Proverbs (chapter 31) who serves her husband and stays home to spin, but omitted from the reading are the verses about how she purchases fields and shrewdly manages merchandise. Cut from the lectionary reading is verse 17: "She girds herself with strength, and makes her arms strong." Only two short readings from Ruth are found in the Lectionary, both on weekdays. The story of Esther is heard only on a Lenten weekday. We hear about Judith only twice in the Common of Saints. Some have suggested that perhaps the violence found in the books of Esther and Judith precluded their inclusion in the Lectionary. But Ruth Fox notes "that principle is not applied consistently, since other violent passages are included such as David's beheading Goliath."[35]

Other Old Testament heroines are short-changed. We never hear Miriam referred to as prophet (Exod 15: 20) nor Deborah's song of Victory (Judg 5:1-31). The touching tale of Jesus healing the crippled woman in the synagogue (Luke 13:10-17) is heard only on a weekday. The account of Jesus' appearance to Mary Magdalene who was the first witness to the resurrection (John 20:11-18) is omitted from the Sunday Lectionary. We never hear of Phoebe whom St. Paul calls "our sister" and "a deacon of the church" (Rom 16:1). Even the Magnificat (Luke 1:46-55), the familiar and revolutionary song of Mary, is never read on a Sunday. While the foundational principle of the Roman Lectionary was to provide readings that disclose the "mystery of Christ and salvation history,"[36] "their selections disclose that they assumed that, apart from giving birth to sons, women are marginal to the mystery of Christ and the history of salvation."[37]

On October 25, 1994, the secretary of the Congregation for Divine Worship and the Sacraments, Archbishop Geraldo Agnelo, announced that permission to use the New Revised Standard Version of the Bible for public worship had been rescinded by the Congregation of the Faith. This decision affected a newly proposed American Lectionary and a Lectionary with the NRSV translation which had been in use in Canada since 1992. In mid-November 1994 the Canadian bishops received permission to continue the use of their new Lectionary on an interim basis until further discussions could be held. As of this writing, a formal decision on the new American Lectionary has yet to be made.[38]

Until a revision of the Lectionary, homilists must find creative ways to include the great themes, stories, and heroines that have been excluded. For example, one can say something like, "It is too bad that we did not hear the rest of the story in our first reading today. What really happened is . . . ." Or, on the Fourth Sunday of Advent (C) a homilist might say something like, "Do you know what follows the last line of today's gospel from Luke? It is Mary's Magnificat which . . . ." A musical version or a dramatic reading from the Magnificat could be included later in the liturgy. While there are many male images of God as King, Lord of Hosts, and Father in the Lectionary, female images of God are few. When they do appear (Lady Wisdom; "Can a mother forget her infant"; "as a mother comforts her child") homilists should underscore their importance. These are not perfect solutions to exclusivity but demonstrations of pastoral sensitivity as we live with the present Lectionary.[39]

6) *A straight jacket for creativity*

There are many homilists who have complained that the fixed readings of the Lectionary are often not preachable. But the fault may not be with the lectionary readings but a misunderstanding of the purpose of the homily. As we read in *Fulfilled in Your Hearing,* "the preacher does not so much attempt to explain the Scriptures as to interpret the human situation through the Scriptures" (20). Perceptive homilists who read and pray over the lectionary lessons early in the week find themselves in places where the sparks of imagination ignite. The major obstacle to creativity is always quick judgment. Instead of dismissing a set of readings as "having nothing to do with our situation," homilists must learn what Jerome Bruner once called the discipline of "effective surprise."[40] Surprising relationships will be encountered by preachers who see, feel, and read the signs of the times with the images, stories, and lessons of the liturgical readings dancing in their minds and hearts. Protestant author Horace T. Allen, Jr., cautions preachers in the "free" traditions not to be quick in abandoning the prescribed lectionary readings in the event of an urgent social or pastoral need: ". . . do first take another look at the readings in that new context. They might not be as irrelevant as they first seemed."[41]

An example of taking another look at the readings in a new context: the Sunday after the Persian Gulf War began, we heard the story of the boy Samuel who lived in a time when "[the] word of the Lord was rare in those days; visions were not widespread" (1 Sam 3:1). It is a story of Samuel believing in the Lord, but at a distance, not closely, not intimately until the old weak-eyed Eli told the boy that the Lord was calling him. From that day on Samuel became his people's conscience because of his nearness to God and his listening to God's voice. We also heard that Sunday (John 1:35-42) the story of Jesus asking those desiring to get near to him, "What are you looking for?" We heard those Scripture stories in the midst of yellow ribbons, sermons about "just war" theories, and Pope John Paul II's pleas against the war. It was a confusing time, charged with mixed emotions.

The night the war broke out, Walter Cronkite rushed in a cab to the CBS news studio where he was called to assist Dan Rather report the frightening news. The cab driver's radio blasted not news of the war but reggae music. When Cronkite informed the cabby that we were in a war, he replied, "So what? Are you some kind of soldier or something?" We live, like Samuel, at a time when not everyone is listening. Not everyone is seeing. At first, the readings seemed not to have anything to do with the international crisis. But with study, prayerful imagination, listening to stories like the one of Cronkite in the cab, the biblical call to listen to God's voice in the midst of hatred and the possibilities of a real "new world order," the readings indeed were timely and prophetic.[42]

Some Conclusions

As we have seen, the Lectionary we presently use in the Roman liturgy is not perfect, but with study, pastoral sensitivity and imagination it can serve as a powerful challenge to the limits and biases of our own personal choices. The Lectionary's orderly reading of Scripture allows homilists an opportunity to appreciate the theological unity of each of the gospels. It has helped restore liturgical preaching to the Church and has had an enormous ecumenical impact. It makes possible weekly gatherings of various denominations for the purpose of mutual reflection and work on homilies.

It should be noted, however, that not all homileticians are comfortable with the Lectionary. The title of Eugene Lowry's book *Living with the Lectionary* is telling. Lowry explains that because of his "non-liturgical" Church background he has a "love-hate relationship with the lectionary."[43] He acknowledges that the Lectionary has produced "substantially better" preaching. But he is uneasy with the Lectionary because its biblical selections are meant "to serve liturgical goals (even specifically eucharistic ones) not homiletic objectives." Lowry seems to see it as a negative that "lectionary selections have been based on a . . . doxological purpose—that is, the lections are part of the liturgical event of praise." Because of the liturgical framework of the biblical readings (the canon within the canon) Lowry wonders "if the selected passages will preach." "That is, are they the kind of selections which will serve the homiletic goal of—proclamation?"[44]

Lowry's distinction between liturgical goals and homiletic objectives appears foreign to the Roman Catholic liturgical tradition where word and sacrament are not two separate entities. Their mutual relationship is found in the *Lectionary for Mass: General Instruction:*

> The Church is nourished spiritually at the table of God's word and at the table of the eucharist: from one it grows in wisdom and from the other in holiness. In the word of God the divine covenant is announced; in the eucharist the new and everlasting covenant is renewed.[45]

In the Catholic liturgical tradition the ultimate mark of an effective proclamation of the word of God is that it leads to thanks and praise because of a recognition of what God has done through Christ and continues to do for us in the working of the Holy Spirit. From that recognition of God's graciousness and the praise that follows we are able to respond to one another and lead the kind of life that echoes the paschal mystery. Thus, the liturgical context of doxology, far from hindering effective homiletics, actually is its saving grace. In his exhortation On Evangelization in the Modern World, Paul VI states that the homily receives its "special force and vigor" from its integration into the eucharistic celebration.[46] The liturgical context of doxology, with the choice of the paschal mystery as the unifying theme of the Lectionary, insures that the homily will remain Christ-centered and that our preaching will be a proclamation of the Good News of what God has done for us rather than a nagging exhortation to good works. The Lectionary has not only provided us with a "richer fare" of God's word but a "richer fare" of imaginative homiletics.

Notes

1. John Reumann, "A History of Lectionaries: From the Synagogue at Nazareth to Post-Vatican II.," *Interpretation* (April 1977) 116.

2. E. H. Van Oust, *The Bible and Liturgy,* trans. John Vriend (Grand Rapids, Mich.: Wm B. Eerdmans, 1991) ix.

3. Reumann, "A History of Lectionaries," 123.

4. As described by Archbishop Annibale Bugnini, C.M., *The Reform of the Liturgy 1948–1975* (Collegeville: The Liturgical Press, 1990) 410.

5. These are the statistics reported by Normand Bonneau in "The Sunday Lectionary: Underlying Principles and Patterns," *Liturgical Ministry* (Spring 1996) 51.

6. See, for example, Gerard S. Sloyan, "The Homily and Catechesis: The Catechism and/or the Lectionary," *Introducing The Catechism of the Catholic Church: Traditional Themes and Contemporary Issues,* ed. Berard L. Marthaler, O.F.M. (New York: Paulist Press, 1994) 136.

7. Pontifical Biblical Commission, *The Interpretation of the Bible in the Church* (Rome: Libreria Editrice Vaticana, 1993) 120.

8. Bonneau, "The Sunday Lectionary," 58.

9. Pontifical Biblical Commission, *The Interpretation of the Bible in the Church,* 68.

10. Lloyd R. Bailey, "The Lectionary in Critical Perspective," *Interpretation* (April 1977) 146.

11. *Lectionary for Mass: General Introduction,* English trans., 2d ed., 1981, International Commission on English in the Liturgy, 66.

12. Ibid., 68.

13. James White, *Christian Worship in Transition* (Nashville: Abingdon Press, 1976) 139.

14. *Lectionary for Mass: General Introduction,* 79.

15. Bugnini, *The Reform of the Liturgy 1948–1975,* 415.

16. Gerard S. Sloyan, "Some Suggestions for a Biblical Three-Year Lectionary," *Worship* (November 1989) 533.

17. O. C. Edwards, Jr., *Elements of Homiletic: A Method for Preparing to Preach* (New York: Pueblo Publishing Company, 1983; Collegeville: The Liturgical Press, 1990) 15.

18. Paul Scott Wilson, *Imagination of the Heart: New Understandings in Preaching* (Nashville: Abingdon Press, 1988) 56.

19. *Lectionary for Mass: General Introduction,* 13.

20. William Skudlarek, O.S.B., "The Lectionary: Too Much of a Good Thing?" *Preaching Better,* ed. Frank J. McNulty (New York: Paulist Press, 1985) 39.

21. Ibid., 39.

22. Ibid., 40.

23. Quoted in Jerome Bruner, *On Knowing: Essays for the Left Hand* (Cambridge: The Belknap Press of Harvard University, 1965) 19.

24. Jan Michael Joncas, "Preaching the Psalms," *Pastoral Music* (August, September 1996) 31.

25. Irene Nowell, O.S.B., "An Interview with Irene Nowell on Preaching the Psalms," insert, *Homily Service* (Silver Spring, Md.: Liturgical Conference, September 1996).

26. Daniel Patte, *Preaching Paul* (Philadelphia: Fortress Press, 1984); Raymond F. Collins, *Preaching the Epistles* (New York: Paulist Press, 1996).

27. Gerard S. Sloyan, "The Lectionary as a Context for Interpretation," *Interpretation* (April 1977) 135.

28. See the complaints of Eugene L. Lowry, *Living with the Lectionary: Preaching Through the Revised Common Lectionary* (Nashville: Abingdon Press, 1994).

29. Sloyan, "Some Suggestions for a Biblical Three-Year Lectionary," 531.

30. Gail Ramshaw, "The First Testament in Christian Lectionaries," *Worship* (November 1990) 502.

31. Ibid., 508.

32. Sloyan, "The Lectionary as a Context for Interpretation," 133.

33. See Justo L. Gonzalez and Catherine G. Gonzalez, *The Liberating Pulpit* (Nashville: Abingdon Press, 1994) 41–4.

34. Marjorie Procter-Smith, "Lectionaries–Principles and Problems: Alternative Perspectives," *Studia Liturgica* (1992) 89.

35. Ruth Fox, O.S.B., "Strange omission of key women in lectionary," *National Catholic Reporter* (May 13, 1994) 13.

36. Bugnini, *The Reform of the Liturgy,* 410.

37. Regina A. Boisclair, "Amnesia in the Catholic Sunday Lectionary: Women–Silenced from the Memories of Salvation History," *Women & Theology,* The Annual Publication of the College Theological Society, vol. 40, eds. Mary Ann Hinsdale and Phyllis H. Kaminski (Maryknoll, N.Y.: Orbis Books, 1994) 127.

38. A fine article, which demonstrates how divisive the inclusive language issue has become between North America and Rome, is Kathleen Hughes, R.S.C.J., "Inclusive Language Revisited" in *Chicago Studies* (August 1996) 115–27.

39. An excellent resource that contains a careful sorting out of the principles of inclusive language, feminine imagery for God, practical guidelines for inclusive language in the liturgy, plus the American Bishops' guidelines concerning inclusive language (1990) is Ronald D. Witherup, S.S., *A Liturgist's Guide to Inclusive Language* (Collegeville: The Liturgical Press, 1996).

40. Bruner, *On Knowing: Essays for the Left Hand,* 18.

41. Horace T. Allen, Jr., "An Interview with Dr. Horace T. Allen, Jr. on the Subject of the *Revised Common Lectionary"* insert, *Homily Service* (Silver Spring, Md.: Liturgical Conference, May 1966).

42. See my homily for that particular day, "Desert Storm: What Do You See? What Do You Hear?" Robert P. Waznak, S.S., *Like Fresh Bread: Sunday Homilies in the Parish* (New York: Paulist Press, 1993) 175–8.

43. Lowry, *Living with the Lectionary,* 11.

44. Ibid., 15.

45. *Lectionary for Mass: General Introduction,* 10.

46. Pope Paul VI, *On Evangelization in the Modern World* (Washington, D.C.: United States Catholic Conference, 1976) 43.

4

Questions Often Asked about the Homily

Teachers can learn plenty from the questions students ask. Questions often challenge and/or sharpen material presented in lectures and required reading. During the past twenty-five years, I have fielded many questions concerning the homily which have led me to compose the following list. The questions flow from the theoretical material presented in the last three chapters. They are not listed in any particular sequence, but as they often are asked during a workshop or class, i.e., one question leads to another. My responses to the questions are offered here as practical and pastoral guides to preachers in their on-going search for what the homily is and what it is supposed to do.

1) *You have drawn upon Anglican and Protestant sources in your presentations. But is there anything unique about Roman Catholic contributions to homiletic scholarship?*

In the past, homiletics was relegated to the broom closet in a Catholic seminary curriculum. It was usually taught by someone with no formal training in the field. Katarina Schuth's study of Catholic seminaries demonstrated that there is a serious lack of academic credentials of those who teach in pastoral areas, like homiletics.[1] *FIYH* concluded with specific recommendations about the renewal of preaching in the United States. The first recommendation on the bishops' list called for "a doctoral program in homiletics to prepare teachers of preaching" (43). The only Catholic institution of higher

92

learning that heeded this recommendation was The Aquinas Institute of Theology in St. Louis, Missouri, which inaugurated a D.Min. degree in preaching in 1993.

Thus, there has been a lack of scholarly homiletic literature in the Roman Catholic tradition. There are theological and liturgical books that contain homiletic implications and also a few homiletic works recently written by Catholics. I have attempted in this work to weave this literature with the writings of Anglican and Protestant homileticians who, in recent years, have produced an astonishing number of volumes on homiletic theory and practice.[2]

2) *If you had to choose the most important question that homilists must ask themselves in preparing homilies, what would it be?*

Let me try to answer that question with a story. A few years ago there was an episode on the television series *Thirtysomething* in which Michael was anxious about what religious tradition he and his wife, Hope, would offer their new baby. When Hope asked him if he believed in God, Michael blurted out: "Sure, I believe in God but God *who? God where?*"

There are many important questions homilists must ask themselves about their particular assembly, the biblical pericopes, the liturgical season, their listeners' "habits of the heart." But foundational to all of these are the questions, God who? God where? In other words, authentic preachers must always struggle to construct a convincing theology of revelation. People who come to church on Sunday believe in God, but like Michael they are asking the preacher, God who? God where?

David Buttrick speaks of the preacher's vocation as a "ministry of meaning."[3] *FIYH* describes the preacher as a "mediator of meaning." The mission of the preacher is not to convince people of God's existence or to explain "religious things" but to unveil and name grace today in our world of limitations.

I have heard many preachers (even young preachers schooled in contemporary theology) who can offer a fairly solid interpretation of the Scriptures and teach the tradition but who seem to have difficulty interpreting our world in light of the gospel. After they say, "The gospel of the Lord," they seem to find it difficult to show how "Today this Scripture is fulfilled in your hearing." Unless we preachers have wrestled with the questions God who? God where? from the depths of our personal faith experience, our homilies will not do what they are supposed to do: lift up our hearts to God and help us live God's new order.

Ultimately authentic preaching springs from an authentic spiritual life. That is where we find who and where God is. St. Thomas Aquinas insisted that preaching is "the sharing of the fruit of our contemplation." A book I highly recommend here is John Westerhoff's *Spiritual Life: The Foundation for Preaching and Teaching*. Westerhoff writes:

> Teachers and preachers require lives that embrace suffering and that are in touch with the depths of existence; lives that are marked by moments of silence and solitude, lived in a rhythm between contemplation and action; lives that are self-critical, that pay attention to the deep restlessness of our spirits, and respond to God's call to grow spiritually; and lives that are lived in a community of faith comprised of persons who see the image of God in us even when we deny and distort it.[4]

3) *Is there a surefire method of homily preparation you can recommend?*

John Allyn Melloh, professor of homiletics at the University of Notre Dame, tells his students, "Method is your friend. It's a help, not a straitjacket." He gives them the example of needing to have surgery: "I would want to go to a surgeon who has a 'method' rather than to someone who says, 'Well, what shall we try today?'"

Preachers should develop the method that works best for them. But we can always learn ways of improving our methods. I recommend a careful reading of the methods outlined in the *FIYH* and the works of Walter Burghardt, Fred B. Craddock, O.C. Edwards, Jr., John Allyn Melloh, Thomas Troeger, James Wallace, and Paul Scott Wilson.[5] Homilists can also benefit from reading books by authors such as Annie Dillard, John Fox, and Natalie Goldberg who offer methods on creative writing.[6] I highlight now what I have learned from these authors and my own homiletic experience.

a) *Begin early with prayer and listening*

FIYH begins with this advice concerning homiletic method:

> The preparation for a Sunday homily should begin early in the week whenever possible, even on Sunday evening. The first step is to read and reread the texts for the liturgy. Frequently the texts will

be familiar, so it is important for us to do everything we can to make this reading as fresh as possible (30–1).

The scriptural texts are meant to be heard. Instead of "looking over the readings," read them out loud. Listen to the texts. Read them slowly. Savor the words. Allow yourself to be startled by the images. Listen to the rhythm. Note the contrasts. Pay attention to who holds power and who is lacking power in the text. Where is the conflict? How is it resolved? What do you find yourself embracing in the text? Where do you find yourself resisting what is in the text? This method of listening to the biblical texts reflects the ancient tradition of *lectio divina* or spiritual reading.

b) *Space out your homiletic time during the week*

Spending quality chunks of time each day of the week in homiletic preparation is a smarter way to proceed than waiting for the last minute to write a homily. Professor Melloh believes that "homilies are prepared in crockpots, not microwaves."[7] When preparation is begun early in the week, there is a chance for "selective perception" to take place. This is a phenomenon where we attend to a certain word or image and then begin to see that object in places least expected. If you have paid attention to the concrete words, the emotions, the images in the scriptural texts, you will find them again in a conversation overheard in the drug store or a hospital room. You will begin to make relationships between the biblical words and images and those found in a newspaper article, a film, a TV commercial, a book, a meditation. At the heart of the creative process is the making of new relationships that at first glance seem unrelated.

Jerome Bruner has described creativity as "effective surprise." But he insists that it is the result of purposeful study or a discipline of "effective surprise."[8] In other words, early preparation sets the stage for selective perception, for seeing surprisingly new relationships which are at the heart of the creative event.

c) *Write freely*

FIYH suggests not rushing to the experts in the preparation of the homily (31). "By doing so we block out the possibility of letting these texts speak to us and to the concerns we share with a congregation" (32). Some preachers consult commentaries and homiletic services too early in the week. This stifles selective perception and thus stops the possibility of preachers stumbling upon their own unique insights from their world and the world of the texts.

One exercise I have found helpful is sitting down in the middle of the week with a pad and pen and writing not a homily or a homily outline but a response to the texts of the Sunday liturgy. I borrowed some of the principles of this exercise from Natalie Goldberg's *Writing Down the Bones*. She suggests that writers should (1) Be specific; (2) Keep your hand moving. In other words, don't stop to reread what you have just written. This is a stalling tactic where you are trying to control; (3) Don't edit as you write. Don't worry about spelling, punctuation, grammar, or even staying within the margins and lines on the page; (4) Don't think. Try not to become logical. Be free to go where your writing wants to go; (5) Go for the jugular. If something emerges that frightens you or alarms you, stay with that energy.[9]

I try to take ten or fifteen minutes writing freely as Goldberg suggests. I write about one of the characters or an image that struck me from the biblical text. At other times, I write as if I were a character or even an object from one of the texts. There are times when I will weave in a snippet of this exercise into the homily. Most times I do not use any of this written material explicitly in the homily. But the exercise does put me into the mood of the text and assists me in dwelling with the Word. It is a writing form of prayer.

d) *Consult the experts*

Toward the end of the week, I do consult the experts. I take about an hour or two to consult commentaries and resources such as the *Sacra Pagina Series*, *The New Jerome Biblical Commentary*, *Texts for Preaching*, *Preaching the New Lectionary*, *Gladness Their Escort*, *Sunday Worship*, and *Homily Service*.[10] I also browse through a Bible dictionary, a concordance, a theological dictionary, the *Catechism of the Catholic Church*. I go to some collections of homilies and sermons whose insights and images provide me with inspiration for the homiletic process. It is reported that St. Thomas Aquinas often read collections of patristic homilies:

> He did [this] in order to offset the aridity which is so often the result of abstract and subtle speculative thinking. He himself used to say that after a spell of this sort of reading he found it easier to rise into speculation, so that it did both his heart good by increasing devotion and his intellect by deepening its considerations.[11]

Over the years I have heard preachers and students of preaching tell me that they slowly abandon consulting the experts because so much of what they read is not used in the homily. Of course, for the sake of focus and clarity, one does not use all the material read, but consulting the experts is an indispensable part of the process of preparing a homily.

e) *Collaborate with others*

In his song "Eleanor Rigby," Paul McCartney captured the sadness of the lonely "Fr. McKenzie writing the words of a sermon that no one will hear, no one comes near . . . what does he care." *FIYH* states: "[T]he preacher will have to be a listener before he is a speaker. Listening is not an isolated moment. It is a way of life . . . It is not just *my* listening but *our* listening together for the Lord's word to the community" (10).

There have been times in my preaching ministry when I have been fortunate to meet with a homily-preparation group. One was a group of priests who met each Tuesday to pray over the readings for the upcoming Sunday. I currently meet with a group of parish staff and some parishioners who gather each week at the church where I preside and preach. The insights and images that are shared in these groups serve as a rich resource for preaching. They also offer us a good opportunity to make certain that we have included the listeners' story in the homily. *FIYH* provides practical ways in which these groups can operate effectively (36–38).

f) *Write out the homily*

Some preachers write homily outlines, others jot down a few sentences with key phrases and transitions. But after over thirty years of preaching, I still find myself writing out the entire homily. I agree with George Fitzgerald:

> The preacher who doesn't write is in danger of becoming slipshod in style, limited in vocabulary, superficial in thought, and helter-skelter. Writing out the sermon . . . enhances the possibility of a sharper image. Writing commits you to words and ideas which have been thought through and prayed over.[12]

g) *Abandon for the sake of clarity*

H. L. Mencken praised the craft of revision that accounted for so much of the beauty and clarity of F. Scott Fitzgerald's *The Great*

Gatsby: "It shows on every page the results of that laborious effort . . . There are pages so artfully contrived that one can no more imagine improvising them than one can imagine improvising a fugue."[13] Fitzgerald remarked, "What I cut out of it, physically and emotionally would make another novel!"[14]

Effective preachers, like great artists, know not just what to put into their work but what to leave out. Revision is an indispensable stage in the homiletic process. Walter Burghardt writes:

> When I think I have finished, I work through every sentence of the homily with a fine comb. I do not need this much on Isaiah, that extra phrase on John the Baptist . . . Block that metaphor, excise that banality, lessen the alliteration. Not a single unnecessary word.[15]

h) *Practice the homily*

After I have "finished" the homily, I put it aside and give it and myself a rest. A few hours before preaching it, I spend some quality time "going over" the homily. I use the term "going over" because I do not memorize the homily word for word but speak it out loud until I can deliver it without notes. I have dubbed this method "planned spontaneity." Writing out the homily in an oral manuscript form helps in this process. The manuscript looks like a script or a written conversation rather than a lecture with long paragraphs. The oral manuscript helps preachers to commit themselves to what they have written and yet allows for fresh and easy delivery. Examples of oral manuscripts are found in the homily snippets of questions #11 (James Wallace), #12 (James Schmitmeyer), and #25 (Robert Waznak).

4) *What is your opinion of so-called homily services or publications designed to aid us in our homiletic preparation?*

We should know that there is nothing new about them. Homily aids appear throughout the history of preaching. Preachers made use of books of fables and allegorical narratives, collections of sermonic illustrations and stories from the Bible and other books plus *parati sermones* (prepared sermons). Sentences from patristic homilies added a sense of authority to the sermons of the Middle Ages. A popular saying of the time was, "A sermon without Augustine is like a stew without onions."

We should not rush to these services early in the homiletic process. The best stories, illustrations, insights are those "right under our nose." One should not substitute one's own homiletic reflection with the finished product of others. There was a popular homily collection in the Middle Ages with the ominous title *Dormi Secure*—"Sleep Securely." The author, Johannes de Werden (d. 1437), wrote in the book's preface: "Sleep securely and do not worry about your sermon tomorrow; there are plenty to choose from in this book." In 1893 George Bernard Shaw wrote *Mrs. Warren's Profession* to reveal the hypocrisy of a social order that glorified profit. In the play, one of Shaw's characters says to the son of a minister, "A curious thing to have to write a sermon every Sunday." The son replies, "Curious indeed. He doesn't write his sermons, he *buys* them!" Homilists who get in the rut of parroting the prepared homilies of others should make an appointment with a spiritual director and/or go on an extended sabbatical. There is obviously something lacking in their spiritual lives.

After a few days of prayerful reflection on the biblical readings and some consultation with biblical commentaries, a preacher may want to browse a homiletic service. The stories, images, and insights found there might serve as jump starters to imagination and prayerful reflection.

5) *Do you believe homilists should take their manuscripts to the pulpit? Aren't outlines easier to preach from? What is the advantage of not using notes or a manuscript while you preach?*

The first response I have to a homilist with a manuscript is "Hooray!" At least I know that the preacher took time to prepare. Some preachers jot down a few phrases or a bare bones outline. Often such homilies lack precision, clarity, and focus because the homilist is actually preparing the homily at the pulpit rather than at a desk.

The other extreme is the preacher who carefully prepares a homily manuscript and then takes it to the pulpit. It is read with exactness, but there is little eye contact and audience rapport. This gives the impression that the manuscript is more important than the listeners. Fulton Sheen once told the story of an elderly woman who chastised a young priest after Mass because he had read his entire sermon. She told him, "If *you* can't remember it, how am *I* supposed to remember it?"

We must find a method that works best for us and our listeners. It should be a method where, although we have carefully written out the homily, we do not let our manuscript or homily outline get in the way of a free delivery. I have learned from teaching homiletics that people develop various methods that work well for them.

6) *In your presentations, you have emphasized the preacher as poet. I never read poetry. Are you suggesting that we quote poetry in our preaching?*

As we have seen in the preceding chapters, no one image captures who the preacher is. We are heralds, teachers, interpreters, witnesses. These images emerged at various times in the Catholic preaching tradition because of particular needs. Since the Second Vatican Council we have gleaned a stunning harvest of theological insight. But with few exceptions, it has been articulated in the abstract and objectivistic language of the academy which is often inaccessible to most people. We have seen how preaching is a theological event but that the language of preaching must not only instruct but delight and move listeners in faith. The language of the poet is imaginative. The language of the preacher often is not imaginative. That is why poetry can help us in our preaching.

Laurence Perrine warned his students not to read poetry while lying in a hammock because poetry's "purpose is not to sooth and relax, but to arouse and awake, to shock into life, to make one more alive."[16] Of course other forms of literature such as novels and plays have the same ends. But Perrine believes that the difference between them and poetry "is one of degree." Poetry is more "condensed and concentrated," has a "higher voltage," and applies "greater pressure per word."[17] Consider William Carlos Williams' "The Red Wheelbarrow":

> so much depends
> upon
>
> a red wheel
> barrow
>
> glazed with rain
> water
>
> beside the white
> chickens[18]

Karl Rahner chided his fellow theologians because they had lost the imagination of the poet and had become hopelessly prosaic:

> Where are those ages when the great theologian wrote hymns as well? When they could write like Ignatius of Antioch, versify like

Methodius of Olympus, when they lived in the ecstasy of hymns like Adam of St. Victor, Bonaventure, and Thomas Aquinas?[19]

Please note that Rahner did not chide his fellow theologians because they were expressing theology but because they did not express their theology with the vision and imaginative language of the poet. Others have followed up on Rahner's plea for poetic expression. Ronald Witherup has suggested a reimagining of the priest (preacher) as poet.[20] The title Walter Brueggemann gave to his 1989 Lyman Beecher Lectures on Preaching at Yale Divinity School is telling: *Finally Comes the Poet: Daring Speech for Proclamation.* Brueggemann proposes that contemporary preaching should be a "poetic construal of an alternative world."[21] His choice of the image of the preacher as poet is based on a conviction that "preaching is an event in transformed imagination. Poets, in the moment of preaching, are permitted to perceive and voice the world differently, to dare a new phrase, a new picture, a fresh juxtaposition of matters long known."[22]

The New Homiletic is a shift from a rhetorical to a poetic shape of the homily. Instead of constructing deductive homilies, preachers are urged to shape their preaching similar to the ideas expressed in Aristotle's *Poetics,* i.e., in a narrative style. Thus, Eugene Lowry describes a narrative sermon as "an event-in-time which moves from opening disequilibrium (or conflict) through escalation (complication) to surprising reversal (peripetia) into closing denouement."[23]

FIYH, as we saw, focused primarily on the image of the preacher as interpreter and encouraged preachers to "turn to the picture language of the poet and the storyteller" (25). Certainly teachers, heralds, and witnesses can and must capture the vision and imaginative language of the poet. But the mission of the interpreter demands poetic expression.

You said that you never read poetry. That's not true. You read the Bible which is a book of poetry. The language of the liturgy is poetic. What you need to do is to savor the poetic language of the Bible and the voices of poets all around us. Gerard Sloyan counsels preachers to read poetry. He is not suggesting that we transpose our homilies into rhyme nor embellish them with favorite verses but that poetry serve us in our homiletic preparation:

> Why poetry? Because it says what cannot be said. It does so by allusion, comparison, contrariety. Poetry plays games with language for the most serious purposes. Preachers have to talk constantly

about God, whom they have never seen, to people who are in no better condition than we are on that score. Poetry helps us do that best.[24]

7) *How do we preachers develop the picture language of the poet? Could you demonstrate a practical way of avoiding the abstract language of the teacher and the herald?*

S. I. Hayakawa was a general semanticist before becoming a senator of California. He often spoke of how we use the ladder of abstraction when ordering our world. At the bottom rung of the ladder is "Bessy." As you go up the ladder, the words become more and more abstract. On the second rung, Bessy becomes "a cow," on the third, "an animal," on the fourth, "a farm possession." At the top of the ladder of abstraction, Bessy becomes "a thing." Now there is nothing wrong with abstract language. It has the noble purposes of classifying items and putting order to our universe. The language of the scientist, the theologian, and the philosopher must of necessity go up the ladder of abstraction. But the language of the poet is always at the bottom rung of the ladder. It is picture language which is subjective and concrete. It is language that not only instructs but delights and moves the listener.

In one of her poems, Anne Sexton says, "I wore rubies and bought tomatoes."[25] Many preachers would say, "I have had high points and low points in my life." Such words do not grip us. They are words high on the ladder of abstraction. We need to capture the language of experience, "rubies and tomatoes."

After you have completed a homily, read it over carefully and check your language. Delete from your homily narrative breaks such as "let me share with you a story;" "next, let me tell you two more things;" "I would just like to add here;" "in conclusion, let me leave you with . . . ." Such phrases break the conversational quality of the homily and are annoying reminders to the assembly that they are listening to a speech rather than partaking of a banquet from God's word.

Read your homily carefully and ask yourself if it lacks the passion of the poet. Robert Frost once said that "every poem begins with a lump in the throat." What moved you to write your homily? Have you captured that passion in your words? Preaching is heart-to-heart talk. If your homily lacks heart, it probably won't move others.

Have you captured the emotion and images of the biblical pericopes? How have you played with (prayed over) the tiny mustard seed, the deep-rooted sycamore tree, Jesus asleep on a cushion, people sucking the milk of comfort from Jerusalem's abundant breasts? Have you ignored these controlling images in favor of dry, didactic language?[26] If so, go back to the biblical texts and chew on these images, feel them, see them, hear them as if for the first time.

Notice abstract nouns that end in -ion and substitute for them graphic images. Be careful of "church chat" that might be the language of theologians and ministers but not the language of most people. How specific is your language? Don't say "flowers," say "marigolds"; don't say "in the market place" but "the corner of 13th and River Street"; don't say "food" but "pastrami and cheese" or "tofu patties." Where are you on the ladder of abstraction? Don't tell us, show us. Stay with Bessy!

8) *Where does one get fresh stories, images, illustrations?*

When you ask writers, poets, or artists that same question, they usually scratch their heads and come up with strange answers. The question was once posed to D. H. Lawrence and he replied, "I never know when I sit down just what I am going to write. I make no plan. It just comes and I don't know where it comes from."[27] When American poet laureate Robert Penn Warren was asked the same question, he replied, "I don't know. All I know is that I never get my inspiration while I'm at the typewriter." Nobel poet laureate Czeslaw Milosz refuses to conduct workshops on how to write poetry because he believes his poems come from some outside force, invisible guests, a mysterious muse. For him, poetry is a matter of being used by the muse. He writes:

> The purpose of poetry is to remind us
> how difficult it is to remain just one person,
> for our house is open, there are no keys in the doors,
> and invisible guests come in and out at will.[28]

The preacher can learn from these responses. There is a mysterious, other-worldly quality to imaginative writing. It is not so much that we are creating a poem but that the poem is finding us. That is why a passive, receptive quality is so vital in the homiletic process. Preaching suffers when preachers are convinced they already know what the biblical pericopes are all about. That is why *FIYH* underscores the importance of "dwelling with the Word" early in a week of homiletic preparation:

> Keep in mind that what we are listening for is a Word from the Lord, a Word which can be heard as good news. We will be all the more disposed to hear and receive such a word if our reading is a prayerful, attentive listening to the text of the Scriptures. Try to read the text without saying, "What does it mean?" Approach it humbly, dwell with it, and let it speak for itself (31).

There is another response to the question. It seems the exact opposite of the mysterious, other-worldly responses listed above. The answer, simply put is, write about what's under your nose! That is the answer of American poet William Carlos Williams. He was also a children's doctor and wrote many of his poems on prescription pads in between office visits by his patients. He glanced out the window and saw what was under his nose and scribbled down "a red wheel barrow glazed with rain water beside the white chickens." Emily Dickinson would give the same answer as Williams: Write about what's under your nose! She wrote in a letter to her cousins late in her life, "Consider the lilies of the field is the only commandment I ever obeyed."[29]

We preachers often ignore what's under our nose because somehow we think it is not mighty or profound enough to be the stuff of poetry or preaching. Flannery O'Connor was amused when someone suggested she should write an autobiography. Why would anyone be interested in her story? It revealed no magnificent adventure, no cast of thousands, not even much of a change of scenery. The invalid storyteller rejected the idea because "lives spent between the house and the chicken yard do not make exciting copy."[30]

O'Connor's life, like most of ours, seemed small and circumscribed. But there was a difference. She had developed the gift of the poet, the artist, the creative storyteller who knew that even an ordinary life contained seeds of depth, of transcendence, of new vision. Nothing escaped her attention, the sounds, the sights, the stories of her short life: the old man Dudley waiting for a geranium to appear in a window; the political chat at the barbershop; the revelation she had in the doctor's waiting room. We preachers often have big mouths. What we need even more are big eyes and ears to see and hear what is around us.

There is much that a homilist can gain from reading the works of others. Indeed, consistent exposure to the finest in drama, literature, painting, music, the media is a *sine qua non* for creative homiletics. But

I truly believe that our best stories and images are those right under our noses. Preacher and poet Frederick Buechner put it this way:

> Christian faith *always* has to do with flesh and blood, time and space, more specifically with your flesh and blood and mine, with the time and space that day by day we are all of us involved with, stub our toes on, flounder around in trying to look, as if we have good sense.[31]

9) *Is it ethical to make up stories for homiletic use?*

There is a deep hunger in our age for authenticity. I see no reason for making up stories, especially when there are so many in our own contemplation of life that speak more loudly to our age than made-up tales. There are times when, because of issues of confidentiality, a preacher has a serious ethical duty to change the names and places of stories "to protect the innocent."

10) *You seemed to downgrade the importance of the image of the preacher as teacher. Aren't we living in a time when people are ignorant of their religion and the teachings of the Church? Doesn't the new Catechism provide an excellent resource for preachers in our day?*

As I mentioned earlier, there is a need to preserve and appreciate all four images in the Roman Catholic preaching tradition. There always was and always will be the need for the preacher to teach. A 1994 New York Times/CBS poll revealed some startling statistics. Almost two-thirds of American Catholics believe that during Mass the bread and wine can best be understood as "symbolic reminders of Christ" rather than as actually being changed into Christ's body and blood. When asked if someone could be a good Catholic if he or she did not believe Jesus was the son of God, 17 percent of young Catholics (18–29 years of age) said yes. Such statistics have caused some worried church leaders to signal a return to the instructional sermon at Mass. They reason that Mass time is the only time to reach most of the people with church teaching. That is why some dioceses have begun to produce sermon outlines based on the *Catechism*. The goal is to present a systematic treatment of church teaching through the Sunday homily.

But, as we have seen, the lectionary readings were not designed around a systematic presentation of the teachings of the Church, but around the proclamation of the paschal mystery of Christ. *FIYH* makes it clear that a "liturgical gathering is not primarily an educational assembly" (18). The bishops' document is in concert with Pope Paul VI's apostolic exhortation On Evangelization in the Modern World which states that the homily is not the same as catechetical instruction. *FIYH* does not minimize the importance of instruction but makes it clear that the preacher is not primarily a teacher but an interpreter whose task is to preach in such a way that the assembly gives thanks to God and is formed for Christian witness in the world. We must learn from our homiletic history that doctrinal syllabi can easily choke the proclamation of the gospel and rob people of their biblical, liturgical heritage.

Cardinal John Henry Newman in his *Apologia* wrote of the *Roman Catechism:* "I rarely preach a sermon but I go to this beautiful and complete Catechism to get both my matter and my doctrine."[32] The new *Catechism* can also serve as a worthy resource for our preaching. There are many splendid quotations from the fathers, saints, and liturgies that can assist the homilist. The question becomes not should we use the *Catechism* but *how* should we use it in our preaching? (Please see chapter 2 for practical suggestions.)

11) *Contemporary homiletic literature stresses the need for each homily to make a single point. Why is that so important and how do we do it?*

Whenever I hear a two, three, or more point homily during a preaching workshop or in class, I ask the listeners to repeat the points the preacher made. Nobody ever names all three points. What usually happens is that listeners will choose the one point that they found most interesting or important to their lives. So, from the perspective of effectiveness, the many point homily simply doesn't do what the homilist wants it to do. There is something disturbing about such a homily, especially when the preacher begins to count the points, i.e., "First, let me; second, I will; third, let me conclude." Listeners begin to count instead of listen. Listeners are also put in the mode of students rather than companions in faith.

The term "homiletic point" is eschewed by the New Homiletic. David Buttrick believes that a sermon needs an introduction, a conclusion, and in between a series of not points but moves.[33] Thomas Long prefers to speak of a focus statement which he defines as "a concise description of the central, controlling, and unifying theme of the sermon. In short, this is what the whole sermon will be 'about.'"[34] If the homilist has come up with a clear, unified, and simple focus statement for the homily, chances are the listeners will offer a similar focus statement if asked afterwards, "What was the homily all about?"

We live in an age of television advertising where messages are focused to sell products. We don't click on the TV and hear someone tell us: "Today, I would like to sell you Folger's coffee, and let me just share with you three reasons why you *should* drink Folger's coffee." The commercial begins with a beautiful young woman tossing in her bed and realizing that her mate is not there. She then smells the coffee he has made downstairs in the kitchen. They both go out to the terrace overlooking a sun-drenched beach. They are drooling not just over each other but the coffee in their cups. In the background someone sings, "The best part of waking up is Folger's in your cup." One point, one focus statement! When I offer this example in workshops, some preachers say, "But we're not selling coffee. We're selling the gospel!" To which I reply, "But they're selling a lot more coffee than we are the gospel." To paraphrase the Jesus of the parables: we can learn from the worldly by the way they are so enterprising and so effective.

I wish Catholics would develop the custom of some Protestants who have a sign outside their churches with the title of next Sunday's sermon. Especially helpful are those pithy, creative titles that lead you to believe the preacher not only has prepared a homily but has done so with a clear focus statement in mind. Thomas Long has written, "The best sermon titles . . . are probably those that orient people to the sermon and prepare them to be active listeners, without either promising too much or revealing too much of the sermon content."[35]

12) *In the old days we were told that we should have an "attention getter" at the beginning of the homily. Do homileticians today still teach that?*

The old homiletic books did highlight the importance of an "attention getter" or a "grabber" at the beginning of the homily. In his homiletic text studied in Catholic seminaries prior to the Second Vatican Council, Thomas Liske named three things every good introduction should do: (1) Get attention ("electrify the listeners or startle them or create curiosity"); (2) Tell the exact point to be explained, proved, or persuaded; (3) Relate the subject to the present audience.[36] Many contemporary homileticians would disagree with Liske's first two points.

First, homileticians today are wary of "attention getters." For example, Thomas Long believes:

> It is deceptive . . . to think that the purpose of a sermon introduction is to snap the listeners to attention. The listeners, for the most part, freely choose to give their attention, and this gift, eagerly granted, must not be squandered by the preacher. Sermon introductions do not grab the hearer's attention; we already have that. It would be more accurate to say that sermon introductions must not lose the listeners' attention, but that wisdom applies to every other part of the sermon as well.[37]

Second, contemporary homileticians would shun Liske's advice about telling the exact point to be explained, proved, or persuaded. This advice was based on a propositional notion of preaching. A homily was shaped like a syllogism rather than a narrative. You began at the top, with the thesis that you were going to prove and illustrate in the rest of the homily: "Today, I want to prove that while God loves us, God also punishes us for our sins." A popular shibboleth in the old homiletic texts was: "Tell them what you're going to say, say it, and tell them what you've said."

But such advice does not hold water, especially with today's preference for the narrative structure of preaching. David Buttrick believes the shibboleth is a "disaster":

> Introductions should *not* give away the structure of a sermon ahead of time in a pedantic fashion. If playbills in the theater were to print a synopsis of plot which we could read before a curtain rises, suspense would be destroyed; we would know what is going to happen ahead of time.[38]

Thomas Long views an introduction not as a point to be proved but a promise to be made: "[P]reachers are giving hints and are therefore making promises to their congregations in the opening sentences of their sermons about where the remainder of the sermon will be heading."[39]

I add here my own observations about introductions:

a) *Be careful of using introductions to "warm up" the assembly*

I have heard too many homilies that begin with a story that has absolutely nothing to do with the rest of the homily. Considering Long's reminder that introductions are promises, it is as if the homilist says, "Get in my car. We're driving to Atlanta." But after the introduction, the homilist takes us to Trenton. A promise has been broken. Listeners rightfully feel cheated.

b) *Avoid the apologetic introduction*

We should be suspicious of preachers who begin their homilies with statements like, "I would like to offer just a few brief remarks;" "I hope you will give me the opportunity to share with you;" "I have a bad cold, so please bear with me for a few minutes;" "I just found out that I was supposed to preach today, so I don't have much to offer." Such remarks do not put us in the mood for listening because the preacher has already presented a weak, defensive, and apologetic stance.

c) *Don't devote an inordinate amount of time in preparing your introduction*

Introductions are often the longest part of the homily because we probably spend too much time with introductions in our homiletic preparation. When a homily does not possess proper proportions, it looks like a monster. It has an enormous head (introduction), a dwarfish body, and the tail of a dinosaur (conclusion). It sometimes helps to cut and paste the introduction you originally wrote, e.g., put it or a part of it at the conclusion of your homily.

d) *Don't always begin your homilies the same way*

The structure of the liturgy is stable and predictable which allows us the freedom and familiarity to pray. But, as we have seen, the homily is the existential breaking through of God's word in the midst of the liturgical assembly. It should not be predictable. There are some preachers who *always* begin their homily with something like "In our biblical readings today God is asking us to . . . ." There are others who *always* begin their homilies with the latest movie or a "Calvin and Hobbes" or "Peanuts" comic strip. The effect is "Ho hum, here it comes again."

e) *Break down long, complex sentences*

Lord save us from homilies that begin like this: "There is a sense in which the readings today protect us from life's ambiguities on the one hand, but on the other hand lead us to the gospel call of building up the reign of God." In the oral event of preaching, listeners do not have the luxury of rereading a sentence to find out what subject went with what verb. Since a homily is familiar conversation we can learn from everyday conversations. They do not begin with long, complicated sentences but ones that get to the point. "Hello, my name is Robert." "Nice weather we're having." "It's good to see you again." A homily's introduction (and conclusion) should contain pithy sentences. Writing out your homily in "sense lines" or in an "oral manuscript" helps keep the sentences tight.

f) *Notice the way other preachers begin their homilies*

Good cooks are always reading cookbooks. Not that they follow the recipes they read with exact obedience to the ingredients and the manner of cooking. Good cooks read cookbooks to jar their imaginations and to discover how others are doing it. St. Augustine said something similar about preaching in his *De Doctrina Christiana:* "Given a sharp and eager mind, eloquence is picked up more rapidly by those who read and listen to the words of the eloquent than by those who follow the rules of eloquence."[40] There are many wonderful collections of homilies from which preachers could learn not only how to begin a homily, but how to develop and conclude it. Notice how James Wallace begins an Easter Week homily:

> The biblical theologian Gerard Sloyan speaks of Nicodemus as
>   "a figure of earnest spinelessness."
> He sees him as one of the learned who lacked the courage
>   to face up to the demands of truth
>   for fear of losing his position or social advantage.
> That's one way to look at him, I'm sure.
> But that's not how I see him.[41]

Listeners naturally ask, "OK, how do *you* see Nicodemus?" They expect the preacher's promise to be fulfilled, and it is.

13) *I usually know how I'm going to begin a homily but I often don't know how to come to a graceful conclusion. Could you give us some hints on homily endings?*

That is why I compared some homily endings to dinosaur tails. They seem to slue around rather than simply conclude. A priest once told me that when his archbishop preaches, some of his clerical listeners whisper to each other, "He hasn't landed yet!" That's another good metaphor for a homily conclusion out of control. It is like a plane circling the airport rather than coming in for a smooth landing. Such circling keeps those aboard the plane quite anxious.

Endings are not easy. We are often awkward in ending a telephone conversation, saying farewell at a train station, leaving a friend in a hospital room. Therapists speak of the difficulty of the last sessions with their clients. They call it "separation anxiety." Consider the following advice concerning homily endings:

a) *Keep it brief*

As with other aspects in life, the best ending is short and sweet. We don't end our everyday conversations with formal phrases such as, "In conclusion, let me leave you with one final point" or "What have I been trying to say in these last ten minutes? Let me sum it up." Since a homily is a familiar conversation, we should delete such phrases from our preaching. We should also strike out multiple endings. Some preachers signal to their listeners by their words and demeanor that they are coming to an end and then go on to add a P.S. to the homily. Again, be careful of the dinosaur's tail.

b) *Inspiration, not lettuce*

Be careful also of salad endings: "Lettuce" do this; "lettuce" try harder; "lettuce" be more loving. Such endings sound like Pelagian war cries. They diminish the anamnetic character of the homily, i.e., remembering what God has done for us. *FIYH* states that the conclusion of a homily can "be an invitation to praise God who wills to be lovingly and powerfully present in the lives of his people" (24). An effective ending is one that offers a short illustration of somebody who has actually done what the preacher wants us to do. This gives the conclusion a mood of inspiration.

c) *Poetic, not cosmic*

Conclusions are often ineffective because they balloon into cosmic, abstract, trite language: "Therefore as we go out into the world today, a world filled with temptations and dangers, let us be aware that . . . ." Make sure your language is specific and your sentences brief.

d) *Reiteration, not addition*

A conclusion should not contain new information, insights, themes but be a clear, crisp reiteration of something already said in the homily. Conclusions should not be designed to learn something new but to feel deeply what already has been established in the homily. The language of the conclusion is "poetic, biblical, and image-rich, matching the affective aim of the sermon as a whole."[42]

e) *Model endings*

Notice how effective preachers conclude their homilies. James Schmitmeyer begins "A Homily for the Funeral of Henry Schlater, Farmer and Friend" with a line from James 5:7: "See how the farmer awaits the precious yield of the soil . . . ." Here is his fitting conclusion:

> He is safe with God
> where there is no more
> "suffering, crying out, or pain";
> where God somehow makes all things make sense;
> where Christ welcomes him home
> and holds him close
> like a farmer scooping fine wheat
> into the cup of his hand.[43]

14) *Since the homily is supposed to lead us to Eucharist, should every homily have a eucharistic ending?*

The *Lectionary for Mass: General Instruction* makes it clear that the homily is meant to "lead the community of the faithful to celebrate the Eucharist wholeheartedly, 'so that they may hold fast in their lives to what they have grasped by their faith'" (24). But nowhere is it written in stone that there must be a eucharistic ending, i.e., an ending that explicitly speaks of the eucharistic celebration. Certainly that is one possible conclusion. But one should be careful of always ending a homily the same way every Sunday. Such conclusions make our preaching predictable and rob us of the possibility of ending in a variety of creative ways. What matters is that the entire homily should be preached in a manner and with words and images that lead us to lift up our hearts for Eucharist and, following the celebration, in our life and work (*FIYH*, 27).

There are times when explicit "eucharistic endings" contain faulty eucharistic theology. Some preachers end by saying something like, "Soon we will be going to the Eucharist where our Lord will finally be with us on the altar." Such an ending forgets the ancient tradition of the Church that the Word of God is not less important than the Body of Christ.

15) *In the old days many preachers began their homilies with the Sign of the Cross. Why do so many not do so today?*

That question was put to the Congregation for the Sacraments and Divine Worship in 1973. The response was:

> [G]enerally speaking it is inadvisable to continue such customs because they have their origin in preaching outside Mass. The homily is part of the liturgy; the people have already blessed themselves and received the greeting at the beginning of Mass. It is better, then, not to have a repetition before or after the homily.[44]

Before the liturgical reforms of Vatican II, what often followed the gospel reading was not the homily but the announcements. Once these "priority items" were taken care of, the priest made the Sign of the Cross as a clue that the sermon was about to begin. *FIYH,* however, reflects a renewed understanding of the homily's place at Eucharist:

> In the first place, the homily should flow quite naturally out of the readings and into the liturgical action that follows. To set the homily apart by beginning or ending it with a sign of the cross, or by delivering it in a style that is totally different from the style used in the rest of the liturgy, might only reinforce the impression that the homily is simply a talk given on the occasion of a liturgical gathering (23).

16) *I have heard some say that since each homily is unique, it should never be preached again. Is that true?*

Yes and no. Since each liturgical assembly is unique to its own time, concerns, language, and culture, the homily should be unique to the specific assembly. It is not just a matter of preaching the Good News but the Good News with and for these people. We have seen how the prophetic nature of the homily was lost when homilies of revered preachers were read from another age. Lost was the sense of: "Today this Scripture passage is fulfilled in your hearing."

It is true that there are the "timeless" beliefs that preachers must preach over and over again: "Christ is risen." "Turn from sin." "Believe in the Good News." "Know that God is with you even in your despair." "God's creation must be revered and shared." "Christian faith grows like a mustard seed." The mission of the homilist is to speak these "timeless" beliefs in a way that speaks to this particular time and place.

17) *What is the difference between a Sunday homily and a weekday homily?*
   Do we have to preach each time we celebrate the Eucharist?

The General Instruction of the Roman Missal (42) requires a homily on Sundays and holydays of obligation. On other days, "especially on the weekdays of Advent, Lent, and the Easter season, as well as on other feasts and occasions when the people come to church in large numbers" it is "recommended" that a homily be preached. "Recommended" is a weak word, especially when #41 of the Instruction states that the homily "is an integral part of the liturgy." Why would you leave out an "integral part of the liturgy?" In #131 of the Instruction, we read: "If there is no homily or profession of faith, he [the deacon] may remain at the lectern for the general intercessions." The weak language of #42 and the possibility of a Mass without a homily in #131 reflects a pre-conciliar time of so-called "private Masses" and also a mentality when the homily was not considered an integral part of the liturgy. Charles Miller remarks, "Celebrating a weekday Mass without a homily is like putting a loaf of bread on the table without cutting it for the diners."[45]

The weekday homily is different from the Sunday homily in length. It should be no longer than three minutes. The preparation time, therefore, is not the same as for a Sunday homily. A reflection on the biblical pericopes as part of one's evening prayer the night before or one's morning prayer before the weekday liturgy should suffice.

18) *Is what you said about the five aspects of the Sunday homily applicable to a*
   homily for the celebration of the rites, e.g., baptisms, weddings, funerals, etc.?

Yes. In fact, sensitivity to the five aspects of the Sunday homily will aid homilists who preach within the context of other sacramental rites.

a) *Biblical*

Each of the rites calls for a homily that flows from the Scriptures proclaimed. The one obvious difference here is that the scriptural texts for the rites are not fixed as they are for the Sunday homily. Couples get to choose prayers and readings for the marriage rite that reflect their experience. A family who has lost a young child might wish to select Wis 7:7-14 because it speaks of an honorable age not with the passing of time nor the measurement of years but with faithfulness to God. The *Order of Christian Funerals* states, "A careful selection and use of readings from Scripture for the funeral rites will provide the family and the community with an opportunity to hear God speak to them in their needs, sorrows, fears, and hopes" (22).

Each of the rites offers some direction for the purpose of the homily. The direction is decidedly instructional in tone. For example, in the *Rite for Celebrating Marriage during Mass,* the homily is meant to be "drawn from the sacred text." But then we are told that the preacher is supposed to speak "about the mystery of Christian marriage, the dignity of wedded love, the grace of the sacrament and the responsibilities of married people" (22). This makes the marriage homily sound like a replay of the couple's marriage preparation classes. The biblical texts and the rites themselves are often overshadowed because of instructional homilies.

James Wallace suggests an alternative. He takes a clue from *FIYH*'s definition of the homily as an act of interpretation and offers another way of preaching during the rites:

> In ritual moments, it is appropriate to allow the scriptural texts to interpret these events for the life of the entire community. The homily is meant to be both an interpretive and an enabling event. The question is: how does this text bring meaning to the event that is being celebrated by this community today?[46]

b) *Liturgical*

The homily is "part of the liturgy itself." The homily should not sound like an instructional or sentimental interruption in the liturgy. The homily preached in a rite should be designed to do what any homily is supposed to do: give thanks and praise to God, especially for what God has done for us in the paschal mystery of Christ and continues to do in the Holy Spirit. The anamnetic and eschatological qualities of the liturgy are found, for example, in the *OCF:*

> The homilist should dwell on God's compassionate love and on the paschal mystery of the Lord as proclaimed in the Scripture readings. Through the homily, the community should receive the consolation and strength to face the death of one of its members with a hope that has been nourished by the proclamation of the saving word of God (141).

The homilist must pay attention not only to the biblical texts but to the prayers, actions, and rhythm of the rite itself. For example, the homilist has a splendid resource in the vows that couples make to each other in the marriage rite. "I take you . . . to have and to hold, from this day forward, for better, for worse, for richer, for poorer, in sickness and in health, until death do us part." Pay attention to these words and to this ritual. They are more powerful than local accretions to the rite, such as the "unity candle" or the presenting of "Mr. and Mrs. Spencer" to the congregation. James Schmitmeyer highlights the eschatological tone of the marriage rite when he observes:

> The form of the words known as a vow, words spoken in the face of all the unknown of the future, is the overarching form of the marriage rite. The element of futurity and the trust and hope it engenders is the experience which everyone at the rite of marriage longs to witness.[47]

Homilies in the rites suffer when they become isolated from the wider ecclesial community. We must not preach in a way that gives the impression that the homily is just for the bride and groom, the parents of the child baptized, or the immediate family of the deceased. John Allyn Melloh reminds us:

> Liturgy . . . celebrates God in a corporate act whose subject is the Church. The Church made present in microcosm in the assembly offers its prayer and praise to God, fulfilling the threefold purpose of sacramental celebrations, namely, glorifying God, sanctifying people, and building up the Church . . . The object of the [marriage] celebration is not solely or even primarily the couple. The wide-lens focus is what is happening to and within the Church *because* of what this couple is doing as members of the ecclesial body.[48]

c) *Kerygmatic*

The homily during the rites is a proclamation of the Good News. It is not meant to be a eulogy for the deceased, a cutesy adulation of a child to be baptized, an avoidance of the mystery of illness for those anointed, a lesson on budget-making and the rules for raising children to the bride and groom. Attendance to the kerygmatic aspect of the homily during rites will safeguard it from these aberrations.

d) *Conversational*

As we said above, the direction given for a homily in some rites is instructional in tone. That is why it is important to underscore the familiar conversational quality of these homilies so they don't become classroom lectures. This is not the time to give three points on the meaning of death or marriage but to speak in words and images that the gathered community will recognize as their own. It is helpful to view the rites as "passage rites" that present the triadic movement of separation, transition, and reintegration.[49] These movements can provide a homiletic structure with which the assembly can identify.

e) *Prophetic*

Once again, *FIYH*'s definition of the homily as an interpretation of life in light of the gospel keeps the homily preached in the rites from becoming a one-size-fits-all. It is the life of this *particular* couple, child, deceased person, penitent lived in *this* culture that is interpreted in light of the gospel. The homily should not be a eulogy about the deceased nor a biographical sketch of the romantic life of a couple. A simple reference to the profession of the deceased, a concrete image that was noticed during the marriage preparation, the origin of the name of the child to be baptized will anchor the gospel in particular realities of people's lives. This does not mean that the homily in the rite is directed *only* to these individuals but to the gathered assembly so that their lives are also interpreted in the light of the gospel and the rite.

There are a number of books containing generic wedding and funeral homilies. I prefer books which contain wedding and funeral homilies that were actually preached on specific occasions rather than the generic homilies for the rites found in some collections.[50] Busy pastors given the charge of preaching many wedding and funeral homilies cannot possibly come up with a unique homily each time. Over the years, they save a few good "chestnuts" from these books and their own compositions. The effective homilist is the one who takes these old chestnuts and warms them up for the context of this particular wedding or funeral.

19) *I still don't understand the difference between a funeral homily and a eulogy. How do you make the distinction?*

The *OCF* states that there is to be a "brief" homily but it is "never to be a eulogy" (27). In the ancient Greek world, a eulogy (from *eulogein,* meaning to "acknowledge") was given in praise of someone who had died for the country. This type of funeral speech centered on the accomplishments of the individual. The reason why the *OCF* makes the distinction is to prevent funeral homilies from becoming a speech of praise for the accomplishments of the deceased. It insists that:

> [T]he homilist should dwell on God's compassionate love and on the paschal mystery of the Lord, as proclaimed in the Scripture readings. The homilist should also help the members of the assembly to understand that the mystery of God's love and the mystery of Jesus' victorious death and resurrection were present in the life of the deceased and that these mysteries are active in their own lives as well (27).

Some purists interpret # 27 of the *OCF* in a restrictive way and end up preaching generic funeral homilies which speak to nobody's experience. But Robert Krieg has remarked that funeral preaching which never adverts to the deceased is insensitive.[51] It is also jarring to most people's expectations. In 1994, *The New York Times* reported the death of Benedict Barnas, the first person to die of exposure on the streets of New York that winter. The article ended with this sad commentary:

> A funeral Mass for Mr. Barnas was offered on Thursday morning at Holy Family Catholic Church. A howling wind drifted snow outside the enormous church as no more than a dozen people filed into the pews. The five-minute homily made no mention of a single detail of Mr. Barnas's life or death.[52]

We must interpret #27 alongside of #5 of the *OCF:* "Christians celebrate the funeral rites to offer worship, praise, and thanksgiving to God for the gift of a life which has now been returned to God, the author of life and the hope of the just." The homilist does not give a eulogy but pays attention to *the gift of a life which has now been returned to God.* William Cieslak makes a helpful distinction between the eulogy and the funeral homily when he writes, "[A] eulogy focuses on the deceased; a homily focuses on the church's story told because of the death of the deceased and in light of the deceased's faith."[53]

Besides the distinction just made between the eulogy and the funeral homily, I add the following observations:

a) *Be sensitive to the deceased's Christian quality of life*

When preaching at the funeral of a borderline or non-practicing Catholic, the homilist should pay particular attention to our God who alone judges human hearts. William Cieslak advises:

> More attention might be given to the prayer of the assembly and to God's mercy and love for all. If, on the other hand, the deceased

was recognized as a very good person, rich in faith, deep in commitment, the service might focus on the Good News of Christ as manifest in the life of the deceased.[54]

b) *Never tell people why someone has died*

Dreadful statements have been made in funeral homilies about why someone died, e.g., "God wanted to take her home." These statements do not console those left behind. They portray a petty God and give the impression that the preacher knows the will of God! A week after his son Alex was killed in a car accident, William Sloane Coffin said in a sermon:

> The one thing that should never be said when someone dies is: "It is the will of God." Never do we know enough to say that. My own consolation lies in knowing that it was *not* the will of God that Alex die; that when the waves closed over the sinking car, God's heart was the first of all our hearts to break.[55]

c) *Pay attention to the mood of the assembly*

Certainly there is a difference between the lament that occurs at the death of a young child and with someone who has lived a long, fulfilled life. There is a difference in the lament that occurs at the death of someone who has suffered many years from a fatal illness and with someone who has died suddenly in a car accident. But the preacher must always be sensitive to the grieving process which loved ones must pass through, no matter what the age of the deceased, the quality of their relationship, or the reason for death. There is still some sense of lament. The *OCF* encourages us to "respond to the anguish voiced by Martha, the sister of Lazarus: 'Lord, if you had been here, my brother would never have died'" (9).

We must not be afraid of lament. It is a prayer, said in anger, said in pain, asking God "why?" Lament, however, does not end in despair but in God who has been faithful in the past and is with us in our present sorrow. A frightening range of emotions is present at a funeral liturgy: anger, relief, guilt, and sorrow. It is necessary to name these emotions even in the midst of thanksgiving to God for the gift of life of the deceased.

d) *Pay attention to the prayers and rites of the funeral*

The film "I Never Sang For My Father" left us with a haunting line: "Death ends a life but not a relationship." The Church's prayers and rites of the funeral are wonderfully sensitive to that belief. They are grounded in a belief in the community of saints. They remind us that the deceased is still connected and related to those who live. The *OCF* acknowledges the pain of separation but also recognizes "the spiritual bond that still exists between the living and the dead and proclaims its belief that all the faithful will be raised up and reunited in the new heavens and a new earth, where death will be no more" (6).

e) *Be kind*

We proclaim the gospel not just in our preaching but in the manner we relate to others and minister to them. It is not just the words of the homily that will speak to the gathered assembly at the funeral but the manner in which the rite is prepared and celebrated. We remember the influence that the preaching of St. Ambrose made on St. Augustine. But Augustine's initial attraction to Ambrose came not from his preaching but his kindness. In the Confessions, he speaks of his introduction to the bishop of Milan and how, to his surprise, he was warmly received: "My heart warmed to him not at first as a teacher of the truth, which I had quite despaired of finding in your Church, but simply as a man who showed me kindness."[56] Kindness is always required of the minister, but it is especially needed at the time of a death when people are vulnerable and emotions are raw.

f) *Be brief*

There is a practical wisdom to the *OCF*'s call for a "brief" homily (141). Enough said.

20) *What's the latest concerning homilies for children?*

Children are members of the assembly of the baptized. Indeed, the assembly is impoverished without them. Louis Weil put it this way:

> Children bring a naturalness to the liturgy which stands as a judgment upon our overformalized routines. Until they are pressed into behavioral molds, they bring a wonderful openness to the experience of word and gesture, touch and movement—to the whole array of elements which lie at the heart of the liturgical act.[57]

The 1973 *Directory for Masses with Children* recognizes two types of eucharistic celebrations: (1) Masses with adults in which children also participate and (2) Masses with children in which only a few adults participate.

In the first type of celebration, the *Directory* acknowledges that the witness of the adult believers can have a great effect upon children. Conversely, adults can benefit spiritually from experiencing the part that the children have within the Christian community (16). Children should not be neglected but acknowledged as an integral part of the Christian community. This can be done directly in the introductory comments (as at the beginning and the end of Mass) and also at some point in the homily. The homily at these Masses is not a children's homily but a homily that includes the world of the child. Preachers, especially those who are not parents, should seek help from parents and children themselves so that the images and experiences of children can be included in the homily. Provision is made in the first type of celebration to celebrate the Liturgy of the Word, including a homily, with the children in a separate, but not too distant room. Before the Liturgy of the Eucharist begins, children can be led back to where the adults have celebrated the Liturgy of the Word (17).

In the second type of celebration, the *Directory* urges presiders to express themselves so that they will be easily understood by the children but to avoid a childish style of speech (23). It also gives permission to one of the adults to speak to the children after the gospel, "especially if the priest finds it difficult to adapt himself to the mentality of children" (24).

Taking account of what the *Directory* says and from my own experience as a preacher in both types of celebration, I add the following comments:

a) *Avoid child-centered liturgies*

There is wisdom in the *Directory's* insistence that in the first type of celebration, adults and children can benefit spiritually from one another. We should avoid, therefore, child-centered liturgies where children are put on display to satisfy our own appetite for entertainment. Mark Searle has described a child-centered liturgy:

> Children are not only heard but seen: the children's choir, the child altar servers (boys and girls), child readers, child gift-bearers, even children ministering communion. There may be a children's sermon, perhaps with the children summoned out of the congregation to sit in the sanctuary and look coy.[58]

b) *Always a homily*

The homily for children is a homily. It is not a cutesy talk filled with anecdotes that make children laugh and adults coo. A homily for children has the same aim as a homily in general. The *Directory* makes it clear: "The final purpose of all liturgical and eucharistic formation must be a greater and greater conformity to the Gospel in the daily life of the children" (15).

c) *Not a religion class*

When children have their separate Liturgy of the Word, it is a time for the Liturgy of the Word, not a substitute for religion class. The homily flows from the readings of the day. The homily is an interpretation of a children's world in light of the gospel.

d) *Not abstract thought*

Homilists should avoid abstract thought or attempts to make a cognitive point. Simply retelling the gospel story or having the children retell the story is often all that is required. When the readings contain dialogue, children can be assigned to read various characters (47).

e) *Stages of development*

Not all children are in the same stage of faith development. We should pay attention to the work of James Fowler's six-stage outline on how faith develops. After the period of age three which he called "undifferentiated faith" come the first two stages: 1. Intuitive-projective faith (ages 3–6) and 2. Mythic-literal faith (ages 7–11).[59] If children do have their separate Liturgy of the Word, provision should be made to respect the needs and capacities of these two age groups. An excellent resource here is Sara Covin Juengst's *Sharing Faith with Children*.[60]

f) *Dialogue homilies*

The *Directory* states that a children's homily can take the form of a dialogue homily (48). Special care should be taken with open-ended questions. Children should not be embarrassed because they gave a different answer than the one expected.

g) *Young pilgrims in the faith*

While children may not be capable of abstract thought, they are capable of spiritual growth. Do not underestimate children's capacity for wonder, mystery, religious feelings. Robert Coles who has spent many years studying children around the world invites us to "see children as seekers, as young pilgrims well aware that life is a finite journey and as anxious to make sense of it as those of us who are farther along in the time allotted to us."[61] Children, like adults, need not liturgical teachers but "mediators of meaning."

h) *The visual*

The Directory for Masses with Children states:

> In addition to the visual elements that belong to the celebration and to the place of celebration, it is appropriate to introduce other elements that will permit children to perceive visually the wonderful works of God in creation and redemption and thus support their prayer. The liturgy should never appear as something dry and merely intellectual (35).

> For the same reason, the use of art prepared by the children themselves may be useful, for example, as illustrations of a homily, as visual expressions of the intentions of the general intercessions, or as inspirations to reflection (36).

Children are naturally curious. They want to know how, what, and why. Puppets, pieces of felt, and brown paper bags are often more effective in telling the gospel story than words alone. In *Filling Up the Brown Bag* Jerry Jordan hides a prop in a paper bag to create a sense of anticipation for children's homilies.[62]

21) *What is the ideal length of a Sunday homily?*

There is an answer to that question found in the Introduction to the 1981 revised *Lectionary for Mass:* "The homily . . . [should be] neither too long nor too short" (24). While the answer is imprecise, it does recognize that there are times when long-winded homilies are simply not appropriate within the parameters of a eucharistic celebration. But it also warns of "homilettes" which short-change the assembly's need to respond in thanksgiving to God's word.

In many Christian Churches, the sermon lasts thirty minutes because it is the focal point of the service. Ordinarily, in Roman Catholic Masses, this length would be inappropriate. In a study conducted a number of years ago in the Archdiocese of Seattle, laypersons settled on seven minutes as the average length for a Sunday homily.

Does this reflect the shortening of people's time span today? Is it the reflection of a culture where seven minutes is the average length of time between commercial advertisements on American television?

I believe that the average length of an effective homily in a middle-class suburban American parish ought to be from seven to ten minutes.[63] There are some parishes, however, where tradition would demand longer Sunday homilies, e.g., some African-American, Hispanic, or charismatic communities. African-American preaching tends to be longer because of its dialogical nature. Listeners not only respond with "amen" but actually preach back to the preacher. Music is often woven throughout the homily.[64]

There are cultures and circumstances when the seven to ten minute homily just won't do. Archbishop Oscar Romero preached homilies one to two hours in length each Sunday at the San Salvador Cathedral. His listeners didn't sleep. They applauded during key points of his homily. Listening to Romero preach on archdiocesan radio, an atheist once said: "I am not a Christian but I listen to him because he is the only one who has something to say."[65]

On November 19, 1863, Edward Everett, a noted orator, was invited to give the key address at the dedication of the national cemetery at Gettysburg. President Abraham Lincoln was asked "to make a few appropriate remarks." Everett spoke that day for two hours. Lincoln spoke a little less than three minutes. Lincoln delivered what was to become one of the noblest speeches ever heard. He not only had something to say, he knew how to say it.

22) *I have heard you highlight the prophetic aspect of the homily. But often I'm fearful of being a prophet in the pulpit. I don't want to offend people or put unnecessary burdens on their already weary backs. Any suggestions on how I should handle my role as prophet?*

The homily by its very nature is prophetic since it is an interpretation of life in light of God's desire to transform the City of Man and Woman into the reign of God—a reign of peace, of justice, of love. The homily is part of the liturgy itself and because the liturgy is eschatological, the homily always holds out a tenacious hope for the coming of the reign of God and a call to change to the way God wants the world to be.

Recent ecclesial statements demonstrate a "new consciousness" of the eschatological nature of preaching.[66] The 1971 Synod of Bishops said that the vindication of justice and participation in the process of transforming the world is "a constitutive element of the preaching of the gospel."[67] This statement echoes Pope Paul VI's insistence that evangelization must "take into account the unceasingly interplay of the Gospel and of man's [sic] concrete life, both personal and social."[68]

While there is no doubt about the prophetic nature of preaching from the Church's tradition and teaching, the question becomes: How does the individual preacher deal with the role of prophet in a liturgical assembly? In his classic essay "Let Justice Roll Down Like Waters: Preaching the Just Word," Walter Burghardt wisely admits that there is "no simple solution" to this question, "no all-purpose push button to activate the answer. Each issue calls for discernment; some call for blood, sweat, and tears."[69] From that essay, the reflections of others, and my own homiletic experience, I offer the following:

a) *Pastoral = Prophetic*

Love and justice must always be intimately linked. "For Israel, the practice of justice was an expression of steadfast love, a demand of steadfast love—God's love and their own love."[70] I remember being told in the seminary: "Wait a year before you become a prophet in a parish. First listen and observe and get to know the people, i. e., get to love them." I believe that is still good advice. After a year with a congregation, they will know from your pastoral care that you are "not out to get them." You will be free to take on your prophetic role in preaching.

A preacher is called by the Church to preach a prophetic word, but the preacher must never stand isolated nor against the community of faith. It is a healthy and humble sign that we are uneasy as prophets. The prophets of the Bible and the great prophetic preachers of history were often reluctant to take on the role. Seated in his elevated *cathedra* (chair) while preaching, St. Augustine reminded his listeners that Christ alone is the prophetic Word in the assembly:

> Do not think just because we speak to you from this elevated spot—that for that reason, we are your teachers. There is One who is the teacher of all, the one whose *cathedra* is above the heavens. Under that One we come together as one school; and we are you—we are all classmates.[71]

b) *Share the secret*

The traditional theme of Catholic social teaching is the social nature of the human person. Persons reach their full humanity only through their relationship with others. Human freedom and dignity are achieved through communion with others. Papal announcements, conciliar documents, and episcopal statements such as *Economic Justice for All* reflect this social reality. But most Catholics do not read these teachings. The Sunday Eucharist is still their prime ecclesial experience and the most natural place to share the secret of Catholic social teaching.

Once again, I am not suggesting that the homily become a didactic lecture. But in the preparation of the homily, preachers must reflect on the struggle of the powerful and powerless, the tension between cultural values and the gospel alternative. All this requires faith and imagination. John Haughey reminds us of St. Paul's homiletic example here:

> Paul looked upon Eucharistic assemblies with an imagination permeated with the power of faith. Those whose imaginations refused to be so fired saw in these Eucharistic assemblies only acts of worship of God in Christ. Paul went much further and saw these moments as times when many individuals were being further joined to one another in a single reality that was both personal and social . . . .[72]

A number of fine resources are available for homilists like *The Pastorals on Sundays,* a collection of pastoral letters of the Bishops of Rome, of the Second Vatican Council, and of the Bishops' Conference of the United States that echo the Sunday readings.[73]

c) *An unjust liturgy*

The homilist may speak about justice and peace and be unaware that the homily is part of a liturgy that reflects the opposite. Clericalism; exclusive language in readings, hymns, and prayers; ministries not shared with a diverse group of people are startling reminders that "actions speak more loudly than words." The homilist is always a liturgist and must make sure that our eucharistic rituals do not block the biblical vision of a just and participatory community of disciples.

d) *Specifics, not generalizations*

We have seen how the preacher as poet speaks in specific and concrete language. Timid preachers sometimes avoid the sting of prophetic preaching by offering general principles which neither excite nor challenge anyone.

But prophetic preaching which deals in specifics can lead us into a mine field. How do we avoid being misunderstood by taking stances and using examples that can leave the impression that we are engaging in partisan politics? Gerard Sloyan would reply:

> There is no direct answer to that question. One explores human questions in all the depth one is capable of—not as a political scientist or economist or practicing politician, none of which the preacher is, but in light of the gospel. The homilist is a public moralist and in that role a public servant. Christian people are starved for a gospel view of questions public and private on which they must make decisions daily.[74]

e) *Not a problem solver but a vision maker*

Walter Burghardt believes that "the pulpit is not the place to *solve* complex issues . . . [it] is the place to *raise* the issues, to raise awareness, to raise consciousness."[75] Paul Scott Wilson believes that the most effective prophetic preaching is the one that provides "dreams of what human society could conceivably be, redemptive dreams that point us in new directions away from the nightmares of the past."[76] Some think that prophetic preaching is simply telling people what to do, i.e., laying down one more thing to do. But what moves us to justice is not a didactic lesson or a nagging moralistic list of what to do. What moves us is a new vision, i.e., the construction of a new world. Walter Brueggemann believes:

> The task of interpretation is the task of the community to mediate the tradition in ways that construe a new world, that permit a new ethic among us . . . [this] requires a strategy through which a new community might be summoned to a fresh identity and a bold vocation.[77]

We have in the Roman Catholic tradition a worthy strategy for summoning a fresh identity and a bold vocation: the inspiration that comes from the lives of the saints. Some rely on the examples of the saints of our time, Dorothy Day, Mother Teresa of Calcutta, Oscar Romero, disciples of Christ who have lived justice. But we must point not just to these recognized saints but to the examples of many in our midst who go unrecognized. And when we do use examples, we should be specific. Give a clip of the person's life on a particular day which exemplifies God's reign breaking through in our lives.

f) *Practice what you preach*

Pope Paul VI described our time as one that "thirsts for authenticity." He urged us to be particularly sensitive to young people who "have a horror of the artificial or false" and "are searching above all for truth and honesty."[78] In other words, we must practice what we preach. Walter Burghardt puts it succinctly:

> Do you *live* the just word you preach? Are you as St. James puts it, a 'doer' of the just word, 'a doer that acts?' (Jas 1:22-25), or do you simply speak it? Does your just word leap forth from some experience of our sorry human condition?[79]

23) *Given the complexity of today's liturgical assemblies, i.e., people of various ethnic and economic backgrounds and also conservative, moderate, and liberal persuasions, how can a preacher possibly attend to all these people in a single homily?*

In one sense this is not a new phenomenon. Ancient rhetoricians struggled with the same question. Aristotle insisted that speakers recognize various types of people with diverse dispositions (rustic and educated) since each "will have its own appropriate way of letting the truth appear."[80] Aristotle believed that of the three elements basic to communication—the speaker, the message, and the listener—it is the listener who determines the speech's end or object.

In our own day we have become aware not just of the "rustic and educated" but the multi-cultural and multi-attitudinal representation in our liturgical assemblies. We must be sensitive to the language, the customs, and images of diverse communities.

Near the end of his life, Carl Sandburg was asked in an interview, "What in your opinion is the ugliest word in the English language?" Sandburg replied, "The ugliest word is [pause] 'exclusive.'"[81] Some preachers exclude women from their homilies by always using male examples. Some never include children or teenagers or the elderly in their preaching. Some ignore the racial or ethnic mix in the pews. The sensitive preacher makes every attempt to exclude nobody from the homily. Frederick Buechner offers a homiletic examination of conscience to preachers when he asks:

> Who are they? What is going on inside them? What is happening behind their faces where they have cut themselves to make them strain to hear the truth if it is told. The preacher must always try

to feel what it is like to live inside the skins of the people he is preaching to, to hear the truth as they hear it.[82]

Of course, one cannot possibly include all groups in a single homily. What we could do is go back to the homilies preached over a year and ask who was left out.

Preachers should also be aware that the themes and insights of our biblical preaching cross ethnic, political, and generational lines. Consider the great themes of the Bible: love, hate, hope, jealousy, reversal, promise, sin, guilt, forgiveness. One of the reasons for the canonicity of the stories and themes of the Bible is their ability to speak to all people. John Shea reminds us the reason why the "stories of Scripture were remembered and today remain memorable [is] because they are similar enough to our lives for us to see ourselves, yet different enough from our lives for us to see new possibilities. They tell us what we want to know and more."[83] Above all, the Bible is about conversion, about seeing life in terms of God's bold order. Flannery O'Connor once said that conversion is "the only real subject of good literature."[84] We can say the same about preaching, no matter who the listeners are.

24) *I've noticed some of today's preachers telling jokes in their homilies. Is this appropriate? What is the place of humor in the homily?*

Preachers who *always* begin their homilies with a joke have a problem. First, they have allowed themselves to be predictable. Second, they probably are insecure and wish to have people laugh in order to be accepted. Third, the joke often has nothing to do with the rest of the homily. It is used as an "attention getter" or in an attempt to "break the ice."

Humor is a part of life and since a homily is an interpretation of life it will naturally contain humor. The important word is "naturally." We are not stand-up comics. We are preachers. The best pulpit humor is the kind that naturally emerges in our interpretation of life and the biblical readings. A prayerful reflection of the readings will yield refreshing bits of humor: Balaam's ass speaks perfect Hebrew as he reproaches his owner. Elijah ridicules the prophets who have prayed to Baal who doesn't seem to answer, "Surely he is a god; either he is meditating, or he has wandered away, or he is on a journey, or perhaps he is asleep and must be awakened" (1 Kgs 18:27). Jesus is playful with the woman at the well. He smiles when she reminds him that he has no bucket (John 4:11). He says in effect: "Buckets, schmuckets! Why does everyone think they need them to draw *living* water?"

It is not a matter of telling jokes but of capturing the humor of our everyday lives and the biblical texts that should be the concern of preachers. Our lives, like the lives of the characters in the Bible, are permeated with humor. The perceptive preacher knows this and through satire, irony, and wit captures the human predicament.

One final caveat: preachers should be sensitive to the power of humor to hurt. Ridicule of ethnic groups, jokes about women, or those containing a sexual overtone may appear funny to the preacher and even to *some* in the pews but not to *all*.

25) *I've noticed many preachers leaving the pulpit while preaching. Is this allowed? Why do they do that?*

The *Lectionary for Mass: General Instruction* restates an ancient tradition: "The priest celebrant gives the homily either at the chair, standing or sitting, or at the lectern" (26).

a) *The chair*

In the early Church a bishop delivered a homily from the *cathedra* or chair since preaching was considered part of the office of presiding, and thus it was delivered at the place where the presider presided, the chair. The chair represented the teaching office of the bishop. Despite this ancient tradition, preaching from the chair, especially while sitting, presents certain communication problems. The preacher is limited in the use of gestures and animation. In large churches, it is difficult to see the preacher seated at a chair. When St. Augustine preached from the chair, his listeners could see him because they had no chairs. They stood to listen to the homily and "the arrangement was quite intimate. People could press up quite close so that the front row might stand only a few yards away."[85]

b) *The lectern*

Here we call on Dennis Smolarski to help us unravel the rather confusing terminology used for the place of preaching: "Technically, the ambo is a place, originally in the middle of the nave, and (usually) at the ambo is a stand (i.e., lectern or pulpit) to hold the book. However, the reading stand is also termed the ambo as well."[86]

Pulpits began to be built when churches became larger. Instead of preaching from the chair, preachers stood in another part of the church. They would climb steps and stand in an elevated position so that people, who were seated, could see and hear them. The pulpit became a usual fixture outside the sanctuary. This had its disadvantages. It indicated that preaching had become separated from the altar and from Eucharist. Preachers looked down on the people from an elevated position.

Lecterns today are located in the sanctuary. Seated congregations can see the homilist. The lectern, like the chair, is a symbol of the authority of the one sent to preach the gospel. It provides a convenient place for the Lectionary to rest opened, a sign that the preacher is a person of the Church's book. Some homilists, unfortunately, lock themselves into the lectern. It becomes a safe niche to hide their humanity. It need not be that way. Used well, the lectern can provide a strong focal point for preaching.

It should be noted that we should use only one lectern for proclaiming the biblical texts. In some churches two lecterns are set up on either side of the altar. The presider uses one of the lecterns while the lay reader uses the other. The U. S. Appendix to the General Instruction of the Roman Missal states: "the reservation of a single place for all the biblical readings is more significant than the person of the reader, whether ordained or lay, whether woman or man" (66, c). In the 1978 U. S. Bishops' document on *Environment and Art in Catholic Worship* provision is made for a "very simple lectern, in no way competing or conflicting with the main ambo . . . [the lectern] can be used by a cantor, song leader, commentator, and reader of the announcements."[87]

c) *Neither the chair nor the lectern*

While the pulpit became a usual fixture in the churches, early pulpits were usually movable. The Franciscans and Dominicans in the Middle Ages preached in many other places beside the sanctuary, including open-air services in churchyards and public squares.

While we find in the normative documents the option of preaching from the chair or lectern, many preachers today have chosen to free themselves from both. For reasons similar to the popular preaching tradition of the mendicants in the Middle Ages, many preachers in our own time have decided to place themselves front and center or to walk in the midst of the liturgical assembly. Two reasons for this move might be:

Personalism. In an age that highlights personalism preachers wish to shed the emblems of authority and "get among the people." Wireless microphones allow them to do that and still be heard.

Influence of television. Many preachers realize that their listeners are more attuned to speakers getting out among the people rather than stiffly standing at a podium. When Elizabeth Dole spoke at the 1996 Republican Convention, she refused to stand at the main podium. Television had impressed upon her the icon of the talk-show host walking among the people.

Preaching neither from the chair nor the lectern has its advantages. If done well, it can enhance the familiar conversation quality of the homily. But there is a shadow side to this format. Some preachers walk up and down the aisle so quickly that listeners cannot see nor sometimes hear what is being said. Too much walking back and forth can give the impression of nervousness and can become distracting.

26) *What do you do on Mother's Day or Father's Day when people expect a message suited to these holidays but the scriptural pericopes don't lend themselves to such themes?*

Some purists insist: "I preach the gospel, not a Mother's Day homily." They have not grasped the significance of the definition of the homily as an interpretation of life in light of the gospel. Mother's Day, Father's Day, and other "secular" holidays are important parts of people's lives. This does not mean that the homily becomes a liturgical dumpster for everything we encounter during the week. There are two possibilities to consider:

(1) It may happen that after prayerful dwelling with the biblical pericopes of the day, the homilist concludes that there is no smooth way to link them with the secular holiday. The images of the texts simply do not seem to connect with the images of the holiday. But there are other options to recognize Mother's Day. A simple greeting from the presider, a prayer for mothers in the general intercessions, the distribution of a flower to each mother after Mass are all appropriate.

(2) Without doing damage to the integrity of the biblical texts, sometimes there is an image in the texts that does connect with the holiday in a serendipitous way. It would be a pity to miss the image because of prejudgment. The greatest block to imagination is a closed mind and heart. The poet is never closed to the possibility "of finding what you didn't lose" (e.e.cummings). If you believe something

is not there, you will not find it. If you allow yourself the possibility of finding it, you will be delighted with surprise. Faith has always depended on analogy. Some of the best analogies a homilist can use are those we find right under our nose and in the days we celebrate.

This does not mean that you will preach an entire Mother's or Father's Day homily. It means that you will recognize that we hear and respond to the gospel not solely in the liturgical calendar of the Church but in the secular calendar of people. I offer some excerpts from a homily I preached one year when the Solemnity of Corpus Christi and Father's Day were celebrated on the same day:

> Of course, there is no direct connection between today's
>   Feast of Corpus Christi and Father's Day.
> But there is a sense in which the image of father
>   is a good place to begin our reflection
>   on the body of Christ . . . .
> I remember over thirty years ago
>   rushing with my brother Frank to a hospital nursery
>   to see his newborn son . . . .
> I've never seen my brother's eyes
>   so filled with wonder and delight.
> He was awe-struck by the sight of this bundle of his body.
> There was a time when Christians looked upon the Eucharist
>   as fathers looked upon their newborn children—
>   they were in awe at the sight of the body . . . .[88]

27) *What is the Catholic Church's position on laypersons preaching the homily?*

Canon 767, 1 of the 1983 Code reserves the homily at liturgy "to a priest or to a deacon." This follows the liturgical tradition that the one who presides is the one who preaches. The Pontifical Council for the Interpretation of Legal Texts ruled that diocesan bishops could not dispense from canon 767, 1.[89]

This legislation, however, has not stifled the discussion of lay preaching by Roman Catholics. Besides the sincere desire on the part of some lay Catholics to preach, there are other canonical norms that keep the discussion lively.

Vatican II, the 1983 Code, and the 1988 *United States Bishops Guidelines for Lay Preaching* provide a theological foundation for lay preaching. Canon 211 echoes the theology of Vatican II when it declares that "all the Christian faithful have the duty and the right to work so that the divine message of salvation may increasingly reach the whole of humankind in every age and in every land." Canon 759 also expresses Vatican II teaching when it states that the laity can be called upon to cooperate with the bishop and presbyters in the exercise of the ministry of the word. This ministry consists of various means of evangelization, among which preaching and catechetical formation are primary (canon 761).

Canon 766 states that laypersons can be admitted to preach in a church or oratory under two conditions: (1) It may be done if it is necessary in certain circumstances or if it is useful in particular cases; and (2) laypersons may not give the homily at liturgy because canon 767, 1 restricts the homily to the clergy. John M. Huels has written that "liturgy" here means "the celebration of the rites found in the liturgical books approved by competent ecclesiastical authority."[90] "The law means, therefore, that lay people may not give the homily at any liturgy, not just at the Eucharist."[91]

a) *If it is necessary*

Laypersons preach when a parish is entrusted to a lay catechist or pastoral associate who has the responsibility of conducting a service of the word in the absence of a priest. Even when a priest or deacon is available, if he does not speak the language of the assembly, lay preaching may be necessary.

b) *If it is useful*

Laypersons are often part of ministerial teams in hospitals, parishes, campus ministries, etc. It is useful for them to preach in order to share with others their commitment to the gospel and their full citizenship on the ministerial team.

Canon 766 gives the conference of bishops the right to enact legislation on lay preaching when it is "necessary" or "useful." The United States Bishops' Conference responded to this canon by issuing its 1988 guidelines for lay preaching.[92] The bishops acknowledge that the work of the Spirit on the local level is demonstrated by the increased participation of laypersons in various apostolates and in a deepened knowledge of Scripture and theology. The U.S. guidelines restrict the homily to the ordained but name some of the other forms of preaching suitable for laypersons: retreats, revivals, spiritual exercises, missions, gatherings of the faithful for public reflections and public assemblies.[93]

The bishops' restriction of the homily at liturgy to the clergy flows from the tradition that the one who presides is the one who preaches. But it should be noted that a homily is not restricted to Mass. It is also called for in various other liturgical rites: in the various stages of the catechumenate; for confirmation, even when ministered outside Mass; at penance services; when Communion is distributed outside Mass; for funerals when there is no Eucharist; etc. Canon lawyer James Provost points out: "The normal presumption is that these celebrations are conducted by lay persons, and for several of these rites explicit provision is made for the replacement of the homily by a meditation, instruction, or even the reading of a homily approved by the pastor."[94]

The 1973 *Directory for Masses with Children* and the 1988 *Directory for Sunday Celebrations in the Absence of a Priest* make provisions for lay preaching.[95] The 1973 *Directory* allows an adult layperson, with the consent of the pastor or rector of the church, to speak at a Mass for children after the gospel, especially if the priest finds it difficult to adapt himself to the mentality of the children. The 1988 *Directory* gives general principles for Sunday liturgical services when a priest cannot be present to preside at Mass. The *Directory* permits a lay presider to give an "explanation of the readings," or there may be a period of meditative silence. Another option put forth is that a homily prepared by the absent pastor might be read by the lay presider.

At the present time in the Roman Catholic Church, laypersons are permitted to preach but they cannot preach a homily because by defi-nition—by constitutive law—the homily is a form of preaching which can be done by a priest or deacon and which can only be done dur-ing the liturgy. That is why normative liturgical documents do not use the term "homily" when referring to lay preaching but such terms as an "explanation of the readings" and "speaking after the gospel."

The restrictive definition of the homily at liturgy as preaching by ordained clergy combined with the desire and the practicality for laypersons to preach has sometimes resulted in poor liturgical prac-tice. For example, an announcement is made that there will be no homily today since Mr. and Mrs. Welch from Marriage Encounter will give a "talk" on the sacrament of marriage. Or, there will be no homily today since Sister Bridget will give a "meditation" after Com-munion. These practices violate our understanding of the homily as an integral part of the Mass which follows the proclamation of the gospel reading. Avery Dulles insists that the priest undertake a leadership role whenever lay preaching takes place: "The priest has special responsibility to see that the word of God is effectively proclaimed and that those who preach and teach present that word faithfully and accurately."[96]

While we live and struggle with the present church legislation and the needs of our times, James Wallace offers the following possibility:

> [H]ave the preacher preach a short homily, followed by comments from two or three representative members of the community. This would have to be worked out in advance, since there is always the possibility of the liturgy of the word overshadowing, especially in length, the liturgy of the Eucharist. But it would make the homily, like the rest of the liturgy of the word, a concelebrated event. A variation would be two preachers giving the homily, speaking alternately. The interplay of two people thinking, disagreeing, amplifying, invites much more congregational participation than a single preacher. Again, such a homily must not become lengthy or overly complex.[97]

28) *I've heard homilists proclaim the gospel reading from memory rather than read it from the Lectionary. What do you think of that liturgical practice?*

I have witnessed this practice and have been impressed with how effective it can be. Homilists who do so demonstrate that they have placed a good deal of time into their effort. However, I have reservations about the practice because of its potential to diminish the ancient tradition of proclaiming from the book of the Church. It could put more focus on the proclaimer than on the proclamation. I do not believe it should be done on a regular basis.

29) *After the homily, some preachers go immediately into the Profession of Faith and/or General Intercessions while others sit in silence before these rituals. What is recommended?*

The *Lectionary for Mass: General Instruction* states:

> The liturgy of the word must be celebrated in a way that fosters meditation; clearly, any sort of haste that hinders reflectiveness must be avoided . . . Proper times for silence during the liturgy of the word are, for example, before this liturgy begins, after the first and the second reading, after the homily (28).

Silence, therefore, is a liturgical action. It offers us the needed space for interiorizing the word proclaimed. This holds for the liturgical assembly *and* the proclaimer. Sitting down for a brief period of silence after the homily is both recommended and appropriate.

30) *Walter Burghardt has told us that for every minute of his homily he puts in four hours of preparation. But preparing a Sunday homily is not all I do as a pastor. Where do I find time to preach quality homilies in the midst of so many other pastoral duties such as administration, fund-raising, community involvement, counseling, visiting the sick, comforting the bereaved?*

Dom Bernard Botte captures the state of preaching in Belgium (and no doubt the rest of the Catholic world) at the turn of the twentieth century:

> The clergy were poorly prepared for the ministry of the word of God by such substandard teaching. Neither the classes of theology, nor those of Scripture, nor those of the liturgy offered material for preaching. The clergy had nothing to say except for moralizing sermons, the kind they themselves heard over and over again. They preached out of duty, because it was prescribed, just as they observed the rubrics. I remember the remark of an old Jesuit priest for whom I always had greet esteem: "Preaching is a bore: you repeat the same thing all the time and that bores everybody." Priests no longer believed in preaching.[98]

Given this state of homiletic affairs, it is no wonder that Vatican II's statement that preaching was the "primary duty" of priests was so astonishing and revolutionary. Previous church councils such as Trent had emphasized the importance of preaching but this was the first time that the Church declared it was the "primary duty" of priests.

All of the duties mentioned in this question are expected in a life of ministry. But central to all of these is preaching. Preaching and the prayerful reflection that precedes it give life and spirit to everything else you do in your ministry. Put quite simply, it is a matter of priority. I know some Protestant clergy who devote an entire day of the week for the writing of their sermon. They refuse to have appointments or attend meetings on this day. That's putting priority where your mouth is!

I have told Father Burghardt that one of the greatest contributions he has made to Catholic clergy is the healthy sense of guilt that he has instilled in them for not spending enough time in homily preparation. But as was described above, it is not a matter of quantity but the quality of time spent in the preparation. Beginning early and spreading out that time over a week in quality chunks of prayer, reflection, study, and writing is what's needed.

Natalie Goldberg, who teaches people how to write, has a passage in her *Writing Down the Bones* that has always haunted me. She is writing about artists and since we know by now that the preacher is a poet and artist, her words apply to us as well:

> The life of an artist isn't easy. You're never free unless you are doing your art. But I guess doing art is better than drinking a lot or filling up with chocolate. I often wonder if all the writers who are alcoholics drink a lot because they aren't writing or are having trouble writing. It is not because they are writers that they are drinking, but because they are writers who are not writing.[99]

"And how are they to hear without someone to proclaim him? And how are they to proclaim him unless they are sent?" (Rom 10:14-15). Like the writer, poet, artist, a preacher has no choice. We are sent. We will never be free unless we follow our call which is to preach. We struggle to preach well not because we have to prove ourselves, not even because we always enjoy it. We struggle to preach well because for some wild and mysterious reason we are sent. We have a gospel to share.

Notes

1. Katarina Schuth, O.S.F., *Reason for the Hope: The Future of Roman Catholic Theologates* (Wilmington: Michael Glazier, 1989) 97–106.

2. See the list of John A. Melloh, S.M., "Publish or Perish: A Review of Preaching Literature, 1981–1986," *Worship* (November 1988) 497–514.

3. David Buttrick, *A Captive Voice: The Liberation of Preaching* (Louisville: Westminster/John Knox Press, 1994) 111.

4. John Westerhoff, *Spiritual Life: The Foundation for Preaching and Teaching* (Louisville: Westminster/John Knox Press, 1994) 38–9.

5. See Bishops' Committee on Priestly Life and Ministry, National Conference of Catholic Bishops, *Fulfilled in Your Hearing: The Homily in the Sunday Assembly* (Washington, D.C.: United States Catholic Conference 1982) 29–39; Walter J. Burghardt, S.J., "Lord, Teach Us How To . . . Preach: From Study to Proclamation," *Preaching: The Art & The Craft* (New York: Paulist Press, 1987) 54–68 and the response to Burghardt's method by Elisabeth Schüssler Fiorenza, 68–77; Fred B. Craddock, *Preaching* (Nashville: Abing-

don Press, 1985); O.C. Edwards, Jr., *Elements of Homiletic: A Method for Preparing to Preach* (New York: Pueblo Publishing Company, 1982; Collegeville: The Liturgical Press, 1990); John Allyn Melloh, S.M., "Homily Preparation: A Structural Approach," *Liturgical Ministry* (Winter 1992) 21–6; Thomas H. Troeger, *Imagining A Sermon* (Nashville: Abingdon Press, 1990); James A. Wallace, C.Ss.R., *Imaginal Preaching: An Archetypal Perspective* (New York: Paulist Press, 1995); Paul Scott Wilson, *The Practice of Preaching* (Nashville: Abingdon Press, 1995).

6. See Annie Dillard, *The Writing Life* (New York: Harper Perennial, 1989); John Fox, *Finding What You Didn't Lose: Expressing Your Truth and Creativity Though Poem-Making* (New York: A Jeremy P. Tarcher/Putnam Book, 1995); Natalie Goldberg, *Writing Down the Bones: Freeing the Writer Within* (Boston: Shambhala, 1986).

7. Melloh, "Homily Preparation," 23.

8. Jerome Bruner, *On Knowing: Essays for the Left Hand* (Cambridge: The Belknap Press of Harvard University, 1965) 18.

9. Goldberg, *Writing Down the Bones,* 8, 70.

10. Daniel J. Harrington, S.J., ed., *Sacra Pagina Series* (Collegeville: The Liturgical Press, 1991); Raymond E. Brown, S.S., Joseph A. Fitzmyer, S.J., Roland E. Murphy, O. Carm., eds., *The New Jerome Biblical Commentary* (Englewood Cliffs, N.J.: Prentice Hall, 1990); Walter Brueggemann, Charles B. Cousar, Beverly R. Gaventa, James D. Newsome, eds., *Texts for Preaching: A Lectionary Commentary Based on the NRSV* (Louisville: Westminster/John Knox Press, 1995); Reginald Fuller, *Preaching the New Lectionary* (Collegeville: The Liturgical Press, 1984); Monika K. Hellwig, *Gladness Their Escort: Homiletic Reflections for Sundays and Feastdays* (Wilmington: Michael Glazier, 1987; Collegeville: The Liturgical Press, 1990); Kevin Irwin, *Sunday Worship: A Planning Guide to Celebration* (New York: Pueblo Publishing Company, 1983); Virginia Sloyan, ed., *Homily Service* (Silver Spring, Md.: Liturgical Conference).

11. Kenelm Foster, O.P., ed. and trans., *The Life of Saint Thomas Aquinas* (Baltimore: Helicon Press, 1959) 38.

12. George R. Fitzgerald, C.S.P., "Preaching From Alpha to Omega," *New Catholic World* (May/June 1978) 113.

13. As quoted in "Publisher's Afterword," F. Scott Fitzgerald, *The Great Gatsby* (New York: Scribner Paperback Fiction, Simon & Schuster, 1995) 203.

14. Ibid., 204.

15. Burghardt, *Preaching: The Art & The Craft,* 66.

16. Laurence Perrine, *Sound and Sense: An Introduction to Poetry* (New York: Harcourt, Brace & World, 1963) 24.

17. Ibid., 10–1.

18. William Carlos Williams, "The Red Wheelbarrow," *The William Carlos Williams Reader,* ed. M. L. Rosenthal (New York: New Directions, 1966) 21.

19. Karl Rahner, S.J., "Priest and Poet," *The Word: Readings in Theology,* trans. Carney Gavin (New York: P. J. Kenedy and Sons, 1964) 24.

20. Ronald D. Witherup, S.S., "The Poetic Vision," *The Priest* (September 1996) 12–22.

21. Walter Brueggemann, *Finally Comes the Poet: Daring Speech for Proclamation* (Minneapolis: Fortress Press, 1989) 6.

22. Ibid., 109.

23. Eugene Lowry, "The Difference Between Story Preaching and Narrative Preaching," *Papers for the 1988 Meeting of the Academy of Homiletics,* Drew University (December 1988) 141.

24. Gerard S. Sloyan, *Worshipful Preaching* (Philadelphia: Fortress Press, 1984) 28.

25. Anne Sexton, "Rowing," *The Awful Rowing Toward God* (Boston: Houghton Mifflin, 1975) 2.

26. See James A. Wallace, C.Ss.R., *Imaginal Preaching: An Archetypal Perspective* (New York: Paulist Press, 1995).

27. As quoted in Fox, *Finding What You Didn't Lose,* 16.

28. Czeslaw Milosz, ARS POETICA? *Bells in Winter* (Hopewell, N.J.: Ecco Press, 1974) 31.

29. As cited in Kathleen Norris, *The Cloister Walk* (New York: Riverhead Books, 1996) 222.

30. Flannery O'Connor, *The Habit of Being* (New York: Farrar, Strauss, & Giroux, 1979) 290–1.

31. Frederick Buechner, *Whistling in the Dark: An ABC Theologized* (San Francisco: Harper & Row, 1988) 103.

32. John Henry Newman, *Apologia Pro Vita Sua* (London: Longmans Green, 1934) 280.

33. David Buttrick, *Homiletic: Moves and Structures* (Philadelphia: Fortress Press, 1987).

34. Thomas G. Long, *The Witness of Preaching* (Louisville: Westminster/John Knox Press, 1989) 86.

35. Ibid., 192.

36. Thomas V. Liske, *Effective Preaching,* 2d ed. (New York: MacMillan, 1960) 134, 135.

37. Long, *The Witness of Preaching,* 135.

38. Buttrick, *Homiletic: Moves and Structures,* 85.

39. Long, *The Witness of Preaching,* 138.

40. St. Augustine, *De Doctrina Christiana,* ed. and trans. R. P. H. Green (Oxford: Clarendon Press, 1995) 4:8, 199.

41. Wallace, *Imaginal Preaching,* 123.

42. Long, *The Witness of Preaching,* 154.

43. James M. Schmitmeyer, *The Words of Worship: Presiding and Preaching at the Rites* (New York: Alba House, 1988) 128.

44. *Notitiae,* v. 9 (1973), 178, *DOL*–1432: note R8.

45. Charles E. Miller, C.M., *Ordained to Preach* (New York: Alba House, 1992) 155.

46. James A. Wallace, C.Ss.R., "Preaching, Special Occasion," *The New Dictionary of Sacramental Worship,* Peter E. Fink, S.J., ed. (Collegeville: The Liturgical Press, 1990) 994.

47. Schmitmeyer, *The Words of Worship,* 84.

48. John Allyn Melloh, S.M., "Homily or Eulogy? The Dilemma of Funeral Preaching," *Worship* (November 1993) 504–5.

49. See Victor W. Turner, *The Ritual Process: Structure and Anti-Structure* (Chicago: Aldine, 1969) 94ff.

50. See the wedding and funeral homilies found in the many collections of Walter J. Burghardt, S.J., the baptismal and funeral homilies found in *Imaginal Preaching: An Archetypal Perspective* by James A. Wallace, C.Ss.R., and the homilies preached at six rites in *The Words of Worship: Presiding and Preaching at the Rites* by James M. Schmitmeyer.

51. Robert A. Krieg, "The Funeral Homily: A Theological View," *Worship* (May 1984) 222.

52. Joe Sexton, "A Fatal Spiral to the Street," *The New York Times* (January 2, 1994) 21.

53. William Cieslak, O.F.M. Cap., *Console One Another: Commentary on the Order of Christian Funerals* (Washington, D.C.: Pastoral Press, 1990) 134.

54. Ibid., 107–8.

55. William Sloane Coffin, "Alex's Death," in *A Chorus of Witnesses: Model Sermons for Today's Preacher,* ed. Thomas G. Long & Cornelius Plantinga, Jr. (Grand Rapids, Mich.: William B. Eerdmans, 1994) 264.

56. St. Augustine, *Confessions,* trans. R. W. Pine-Coffin (New York: Penguin Books, 1961) 5:13, 107.

57. Louis Weil, *Sacraments & Liturgy: The Outward Signs* (Oxford, England: Basil Blackwell Publisher, 1983) 81.

58. Mark Searle, "Children in the Assembly of the Church," *Children in the Assembly of the Church,* eds. Eleanor Bernstein, C.S.J., and John Brooks-Leonard (Chicago: Liturgical Training Publications, 1992) 41.

59. James W. Fowler, *Stages of Faith: The Psychology of Human Development and the Quest for Meaning* (San Francisco: Harper & Row, 1981) 119–50.

60. Sara Covin Juengst, *Sharing Faith with Children: Rethinking the Children's Sermon* (Louisville: Westminster/John Knox Press, 1994) 46–52.

61. Robert Coles, *The Spiritual Life of Children* (Boston: Houghton Mifflin, 1990) xvii.

62. Jerry M. Jordan, *Filling Up the Brown Bag: A Children's Sermon How-To Book* (New York: Pilgrim Press, 1987).

63. See Charles E. Miller, *Ordained to Preach.* Miller writes that the "Sunday homily is to be about seven minutes and should not exceed ten" (155). See also

John F. Baldovin, S.J., "The Nature and Function of the Liturgical Homily," *The Way: Supplement* (Spring 1990). Baldovin opts for "seven to nine minutes" (96).

64. See Henry H. Mitchell, *Celebration and Experience in Preaching* (Nashville: Abingdon Press, 1990).

65. As reported by Virgil Elizondo, "Afterword," *A Martyr's Message of Hope: Six Homilies by Archbishop Oscar Romero* (Kansas City, Mo.: Celebration Books, 1981) 169.

66. The words "new consciousness" are used by the International Theological Commission's "Human Development and Christian Salvation" IV (1976) *Origins* (November 3, 1977) 311.

67. 1971 Synod of Bishops, *De justitia in mundo* (Vatican Press, 1971) Introduction, 5.

68. Pope Paul VI, *On Evangelization in the Modern World* (Washington, D.C.: United States Catholic Conference, 1976) 29.

69. Burghardt, *Preaching,* 134.

70. Ibid., 124.

71. St. Augustine, *Sermo* 301A, trans. William Harmless, S.J., *Augustine and the Catechumenate* (Collegeville: The Liturgical Press, 1995) 167–8.

72. John Haughey, S.J., "The Eucharist and Intentional Communities," *Alternative Futures for Worship,* vol. 31 *Eucharist,* Bernard Lee, ed. (Collegeville: The Liturgical Press, 1987) 57.

73. Jacquelyn S. Graham, *The Pastorals on Sundays* (Chicago: Liturgy Training Publications, 1990).

74. Sloyan, *Worshipful Preaching,* 66.

75. Walter J. Burghardt, S.J., "Preaching, Role of," *The New Dictionary of Catholic Social Thought,* Judith A. Dwyer, ed. (Collegeville: The Liturgical Press, 1994) 779.

76. Paul Scott Wilson, *Imagination of the Heart: New Understandings in Preaching* (Nashville: Abingdon Press, 1988) 198.

77. Walter Brueggemann, "The Social Nature of the Biblical Text for Preaching," *Preaching As a Social Act: Theology & Practice,* Arthur Van Seters, ed. (Nashville: Abingdon Press, 1988) 142.

78. Pope Paul VI, *On Evangelization in the Modern World,* 57.

79. Burghardt, *Preaching: The Art & the Craft,* 138.

80. Aristotle, *Rhetoric,* trans. W. Rhys Roberts (New York: The Modern Library, 1954) book l, chapter 7: 27, 178.

81. As reported in Fred B. Craddock, *Preaching* (Nashville: Abingdon Press, 1985) 167–8.

82. Frederick Buechner, *Telling the Truth: The Gospel as Tragedy, Comedy and Fairy Tale* (New York: Harper and Row, 1977) 8.

83. John Shea, *Stories of Faith* (Chicago: Thomas More Press, 1980) 89.

84. As quoted in Jill P. Baumgaertner, *Flannery O'Connor: A Proper Scaring* (Wheaton, Ill.: Harold Shaw, 1988) 2.

85. Harmless, *Augustine and the Catechumenate,* 168.

86. Dennis C. Smolarski, S.J., *Liturgical Literacy: From Anamnesis to Worship* (New York: Paulist Press, 1990) 57.

87. "Environment and Art in Catholic Worship," Elizabeth Hoffman, ed., *The Liturgy Documents: A Parish Resource,* 3d ed. (Chicago: Liturgy Training Publications, 1991) #75, 332.

88. Robert P. Waznak, S.S., *Like Fresh Bread: Sunday Homilies in the Parish* (New York: Paulist Press, 1993) 257–8.

89. Reply, May 26, 1987, *Communicationes* 19 (1987) 261.

90. John M. Huels, *Disputed Questions in the Liturgy Today* (Chicago: Liturgical Training Publications, 1988) 26.

91. John M. Huels, *More Disputed Questions in the Liturgy* (Chicago: Liturgical Training Publications, 1996) 183.

92. The National Council of Bishops' first policy on lay preaching was not approved by the Holy See. The NCCB's second attempt to adopt guidelines for lay preaching failed to get the necessary two-thirds vote of conference members.

93. See *Origins* (December 1, 1988) 402.

94. James H. Provost, "Lay Preaching and Canon Law in a Time of Transition," *Preaching and the Non-Ordained: An Interdisciplinary Study,* Nadine Foley, O.P., ed. (Collegeville: The Liturgical Press, 1983) 143.

95. Congregation for Divine Worship, Directory for Masses with Children, *Pueros baptizatos,* 24, November 1, 1973, *AAS* 66 (1974) 30–46; *DOL* 2157; Congregation for Divine Worship, Directory for Sunday Celebrations in the Absence of a Priest, *Christi Ecclesia,* 43, May 22, 1988, prot. n. 691/86.

96. Avery Dulles, S.J., *The Priestly Office: A Theological Reflection* (New York: Paulist Press, 1997) 29.

97. James A. Wallace, C.Ss.R., "Guidelines for Preaching by the Laity: Another Step Backward?" *America* (September 9–16, 1989) 141.

98. Bernard Botte, O.S.B., *From Silence to Participation: An Insider's View of Liturgical Renewal,* trans. John Sullivan, O.C.D. (Washington, D.C., 1988) 7.

99. Goldberg, *Writing Down the Bones,* 39.

Index